THE ART OF SWIMMING
AND THE
GAME OF RACING

Reflections of a USA Swimming Club Coach

by Dudley Duncan

The Art of Swimming and the Game of Racing: Reflections of a USA Swimming Club Coach

Author: Dudley Duncan
Editor: Taylor Brien
Proofreader: Lyda Rose Haerle
Book design provided by Nicole Wurtele.
All photos courtesy of Dudley Duncan unless otherwise noted.
Illustrations by Anastasia Carneal.

Published by CG Sports Publishing

A Division of The CG Sports Company
cgsportspublishing.com

ISBN: 979-8-9881891-0-7

Quantity order requests can be emailed to:

Publishing@cgsportsmanagement.com

Printed in The United States of America

Dedicated to All of the Swimmers Who Let Me Coach Them
AND
My Loved Ones Who Let Me Coach!

—— Praise for *The Art of Swimming*

"Dudley has been a mentor and friend for decades. He is a legend in the art of coaching the sport of swimming and I am honored to have learned from the best in this book. Dudley draws from his own experiences to offer insightful guidance for developing athletes' and team consciousness, for owning your own business, and for finding the balance between the two. This is an excellent resource for coaches at every level, not just in swimming, but in all sports."

– John Smithson, Head Coach/Co-Owner, QUEST Swimming

"WOW! Dudley has written a great book for aspiring swim coaches, entrepreneurs, and self-starters. Although I've known Dudley for 30+ years, I still learn more and more about his life experiences with the turn of every page. This book is packed with great educational lessons, but also has a ton of great stories and anecdotes told by one of my favorite storytellers. A must read for swimmers, coaches, swim team parents, and fans of sport and athletics!"

– Chad Onken, American Swimming Coaches Association Director of International Clinics

"Dudley Duncan has been a leader in all areas of the aquatic profession. I first met Dudley in the fall of 1981 when I was just beginning a career in coaching swimming at the year-round level. It was immediately evident that this man had a passion for what he was doing, a work ethic to make it happen, and a dream of what could happen.

In this book, I really feel that Dudley has laid out a model for all other coaches to learn from. This book educates people on how to develop a personal philosophy that leads to success in coaching and life. From fundamental technique and training, to developing a team culture with swimmers and parents, to learning how to control your own destiny as an entrepreneur. This is a handbook on how to create and nurture a successful aquatic business while maintaining your own personal values. This is the book I wish I had 40 years ago!"

– J. J. Bean, coach, teacher, sports psychologist, lifelong learner

Table of Contents

x

Foreword

Try on your wings and find out where it's at.

It can start with an idea. It can start with a bet. It can start with a passion turned obsession. For me it started with a song. Starting your own business can be daunting as well as exciting, rewarding, and tiring but it's never boring. "The Golden Road (To Unlimited Devotion)" is one of those songs that just sticks in your head. And for me, as a lifelong fan of the Grateful Dead, this song led me through many unknown journeys. This song changed my life and the lives of those around me. This song inspired me to change my own destiny.

For almost thirty years I have known (or known of) and admired Dudley Duncan.

Dudley was on a hiatus from club coaching when I was swimming in high school at Poseidon. Coming home from a successful first swim season at Yale, I took a risk to join Dudley at QUEST, a risk that paid off for the past 20 years in swimming and business. That summer, Dudley told me I had to rebuild my "backward" stroke in order to improve and see efficiency in swimming that would help realize my potential. After a successful college swim year, starting over on all 4 strokes seemed impossible and improbable, but after countless hours striving for technical perfection, we got there. Not only did my stroke change for the better, but my connection to the movement of water would forever change.

Throughout my college years and after, Dudley instilled in me a love for the process – the journey we call life – and how to both appreciate and anticipate life's biggest grinds, pitfalls, and challenges. I learned it's all about perspective. These lessons helped me build a successful career as an entrepreneur and business leader. They also helped me appreciate and embrace life's toughest moments to make me a stronger woman and partner to those around me.

Our conversations about swimming, technique, opportunity, and life were always rich and insightful. So when Dudley asked me if I would write the foreword to his new book, I felt both privileged and nervous, having never done anything like this before. The passion for swimming with which Dudley speaks, and his evident desire and encouragement for coaches across the country to take ownership of their destiny by taking greater charge of the business of swimming, is evident throughout this book. As someone who has taken on the risk of starting out on their own and shaping their own path, I can confirm it is very rewarding, though challenging at times. Learning to embrace the grind helps us reach beyond what we thought was our true potential.

By laying out his own journey in detail, the lessons he learned along the way and the do-overs he wished he had, Dudley has created a helpful and insightful guide to winning in the sport of swimming, and to encourage those interested in the business of swimming to take more control over their destiny. Coaching swimming is hard work, but why not be in the driver's seat for the journey? Coaches have the ability to lead, shape, and create positive outcomes for those around them AND themselves.

Imagine leading the journey in the way most true to your own personal values. The results you dream of, delivered in the way that is most true to your vision. As someone who has carved a path in an industry dominated by decades-old practices and demographics that suggest a young woman would be destined to fail, I can relate. But more importantly, I know the value of integrating your personal values and beliefs as the North-star to a business model that you find so exciting, it doesn't feel like you are coming to work every day. Instead, you are creating something for yourself and others, something born of a passion you have for a sport or an industry, but that now is managed in the way most true to yourself. That is particularly liberating. Dudley's chronology of his journey is an invaluable source to any coach thinking of taking that first step to become a leader and innovator in the business of swimming. And why not? Even the biggest things have small beginnings.

When I look back now, I see how the discipline, strategic thinking, effort, practice, and commitment that sits at the heart of the sport we all love, prepared me for a life in business. Amazing people in our sport, like Dudley, who shaped so many of us in our formative years, have so much wise counsel to offer, and I hope people embrace this book in that spirit. To quote another line from that song that started it all for me....

Nobody's finished, we ain't even begun.

Meg Gill
08.12.22

Notes about Meg Gill: HIgh School Valedictorian; Yale Swim Team Captain; Started a brewery called Golden Road Brewing, which she sold to Anheuser-Busch; selected by Forbes Magazine as a Top 30 Under 30 entrepreneur.

Introduction — A Quest

When I was nine, I spent part of a summer with my Aunt Marion and Uncle Hood in Miami, Florida. While there, they enrolled me into a beginner swim lesson class—which I failed. I failed because, while I would swim across the pool in 4 feet of water, I would not swim across the pool at the deep end of the pool. It seems interesting to me that from this introduction to swimming, I became a career competitive swimming coach.

When I was 11 years old, my dad died of a heart attack while stationed in Okinawa, Japan (July 23, 1959). Our family lived in the Glendale neighborhood in Newport News, Virginia, while Dad was stationed in Okinawa. We moved to Stoneybrook Estates (Newport News) after Dad died because Stoneybrook had a neighborhood swimming pool. Stoneybrook was also close to Ft. Eustis where my mother worked.

A new competitive summer swim league was introduced in Newport News the year before I moved to Stoneybrook. There were two teams: Stoneybrook Country Club and the James River Country Club.

Mom thought "the pool" would be a good place for us to be during the days of summer, while she worked and we were out of school. And—that is what we did. We were at the pool most of every day during the summers.

There were four teams during my first summer at Stoneybrook. My friends encouraged me to swim on the team, but I was apprehensive because I felt too slow to race. My "friends" would challenge me to races – and they allowed me to win. So I joined the swim team. Then all of my "friends" beat me at races in swim meets.

However, by the end of the summer when I was 12 years old,

I placed 2nd in the 50-yard freestyle at the Newport News City Championships.

I was coached by Jim Maxwell and Amos West at Stoneybrook until I was 17. Both were good men and good motivators. Jim Maxwell taught us racing techniques that he was learning as a college swimmer at Randolph Macon College. He taught me an underwater sequence for breaststroke before others in the league knew the technique. I became the fastest breaststroker right away by using it, until others learned the technique.

I attended Augusta Military Academy (AMA), starting in January of 1963. Mom thought I needed additional male guidance because I was "acting out" a bit. A neighbor was attending AMA so I went there. AMA was probably more male guidance than I needed, but I finished my high school years there, graduating in June of 1965

I swam for Augusta during my junior and senior years (team captain). I wrestled in the same season there. Lt. Marks was the swim team coach at Augusta. He was a good fellow. Capt. McClellan was the wrestling coach, and he was tough as nails.

I was able to qualify for, and attend, the Eastern Interscholastic Swim Championships at Lawrenceville Prep in Lawrenceville, New Jersey. Fork Union Military Academy, located just outside of Richmond, Virginia won the championship in my senior year.

At 16 years old, my coaching career unknowingly began. Peggy Shaughnessy (a Stoneybrook swimmer) asked me to watch her freestyle to see if there was something that she could improve. I saw something, suggested it, and she improved significantly. I began to realize I could see and understand human movement related to sports. I began to analyze sports movement in general as an interest. I could do it for myself as well, and it was helping me to be a fair athlete overall.

I love to observe movement, and have for as long as I can remember. In the beginning, I loved to feel it. I loved to run, and I was constantly challenging friends to foot races. To this day, I can tell when I'm efficient and when I am not.

Eventually, I studied physical education. I applied my studies to my own experience. I also applied it to swimmers I was coaching while in college. During my career as a competitive swimming coach, I have always considered that I could see (water) movement in a different way than many others see it.

———

Academically, my results were pretty good through middle school. I skipped the 3rd grade, which caused me to be young and (immature) for my grade. Academic results were not good during my high school years. I think that it was because I was slightly rebellious. As I stated earlier, Mom thought I could benefit from more "male guidance" so I attended, or was sent to, Augusta Military Academy from my 15th birthday through graduation.

Actually, my analysis now, is that I had this problem of wanting my teachers to be according to my wishes. That is, when I liked a teacher, I would think that the teacher was a good teacher. Likewise, if I did not care for the teacher, my impression would be that the teacher was not good. This approach was causing me to achieve poorly on the basis of my "illusions." This was somewhat true when applied to my coaches too, but not as much so. Anyway, I finally overcame this "personal problem" and achieved well (later) in college and graduate school.

On paper, my education has been pretty extensive: 203 undergraduate hours and 30 graduate hours at 7 colleges. Those are just hours that I had on my transcript. The best teacher in my memory was Captain James Flanagan at Augusta Military Academy. I had Captain Flanagan for American & English Literature during my senior year at Augusta Military Academy, and he taught me many things despite my rebelliousness and ignorance.

Captain Flanagan was a master of the English language. He (mostly) seemed to act out his classes. By using changes in tone, volume, passion, and reverence for the English language, his speech was often such that I would miss some content in the material he was teaching because I was enthused by the manner of his speech.

He assigned an (almost) impossible term paper to me, for some reason which I will never understand. It was titled "The Historical and Literary Events Leading Up to and Including the King James Translation of the Bible." It took the entire senior year to write, and to be acceptable to Capt. Flanagan. With this time and effort, his ability to articulate concepts and information were further ingrained into my consciousness. The history of the time of King James, the books of the Bible (included in the version and not), literature and opinions about them, and biblical references were, in total, a unique learning experience which is effective to the present day.

Anyway, my reason for sharing this story is that James Flanagan taught me to communicate in such a way as to keep interest in a group when the material might not do so on its own. He was a major influence on my life and for my career.

Another great teacher was Dr. Vernon Stumpf, who taught history and government at Campbell College (now Campbell University) in Buies Creek, North Carolina. Dr. Stumpf taught on the basis of cause and effect. He was not interested in having his students memorize dates and events in history. Rather, he wanted us to know the cause or the effect of events in history. He taught that way, and he tested that way. Never before nor since have (history) teachers taken that approach for me. This was another teacher who pulled me out of my rebelliousness and ignorance to learn.

It is significant to me because now I think of movement in that way also; that is, movement does not happen in and of itself, according to individual body parts. It is connected. There is cause and effect.

I was also blessed to have Dr. Melvin Williams for exercise physiology, and Dr. Jerry George for kinesiology while at Old Dominion University. Both were dedicated to their respective fields, authors, and great teachers. Each of them provided me with a foundation of information which I have used throughout my career during 50-plus years of coaching.

One last example of this relates to my experience taking Spanish in school. I took the classes to pass tests, but I failed to learn to converse in it, like many kids who take language(s). As a student (1963 – 1965), I actually never thought I would use it; however, while in the Air Force (1970), I was stationed in the country of Panama. Then I really wished that I would have been able to converse in the Spanish language. This was a moment where it became clear to me that you never know when your education can serve you in life.

The reason for pointing this out is that one never knows how information will affect you. Be willing to learn from everybody that is tasked (or wants) to teach you. Do not waste your time by forming a judgment of a teacher and learning – or not – based on your judgment. Be open-minded. Learn the material regardless. It will not hurt you to learn. One never knows how information will help you at some point.

———

In June 1968, I was hired to coach the Glendale Gators. I was an assistant coach to Bill Nixon, and I made an extra $5 per week added onto my lifeguard pay ($1.25 per hour). We had a great time. It was the "game of racing" that enthused me in the beginning. I did not have real information for coaching at that stage of my life, (other than my personal experience as a summer/high school swimmer) but it was great fun to motivate swimmers to win races.

I was drafted into military service in June of that summer. I joined the United States Air Force rather than enter the Army draft.

My entry date into the USAF was November 18, 1968. This was at the height of the VietNam War. Most men who were drafted into the Army at that time were immediately placed with infantry and sent to Southeast Asia. Rather than accept the draft, I joined the US Air Force for 4 years. I was trained in radio communications, and my job for three years was to "flight-follow" aircraft from the USA to Europe while I was stationed at Andrews AFB in Maryland and back—and later from the USA to South America and back while I was stationed in Panama.

I was reassigned to a different career field during my last year: the Security Police. While investigating a vandalism at a colonel's home on Pope AFB in Fayetteville, North Carolina, we discussed his 5 children who swam for the Ft. Bragg Aquadragons. He told me that they needed an assistant coach, and I told him that I could do that because I had been a swimmer and a swimming coach (for a summer). He executed a transfer to Army Special Services, and I coached the Aquadragons, as assistant to Grant Maas who was an Army guy, for a year. With this experience, I was truly committed to a coaching life; however, it wasn't necessarily coaching swimming. I favored the sport of wrestling to this point. But I was sure that I wanted to engage in a curriculum of learning that would lead to coaching. That was physical education.

I was discharged from the Air Force in September of 1972. I enrolled in Thomas Nelson Community College with hopes of achieving a grade point average that would allow me to be accepted at the College of William & Mary. My GPA was 3.88, but I was not accepted to W & M. Some say "things happen for a reason," and this was such an occasion in my life. I attended Old Dominion University. The ODU staff in Physical Education was excellent and did a wonderful job of preparing me for my chosen field.

During my first year at ODU I was required to take a course in swimming. This class was taught by the ODU swim team coach. He approached me to join the swim team, which I did. He retired after my first year and Mary Fleet was hired as the swim team coach. Mary was a HIGHLY accomplished swimmer at ODU and is now in the ODU Hall of Fame as a swimmer. During that year, she approached me to assist her in starting a "university outreach" swim team of school-aged swimmers.

This team was a combination of a university outreach program called the Bounty program, and a team from the Oceana Naval Base in Norfolk called the Oceana Otters. Thus, this team was called the Bounty Otters Swim Club. Mary Fleet, an inspirational competitive swimmer and coach, moved to California the next year,and I accepted the job as head coach for BOSC.

In September of 1975, I started my student teaching experience at Maury High School in Norfolk, Virginia. At this time, I still intended to teach high school and coach wrestling. But as "things" happen, high school teaching did not agree with me. The fact of this matter seemed (to me) that the swimmers I was coaching had a greater interest in learning than many (too many) of the students that I was teaching at Maury High School at the time.

I graduated from ODU undergraduate in December 1975. I continued to coach BOSC through March of 1976. Three swimmers qualified for USA Junior Nationals that season: Penny Shelor, Joanie Elmore, and Dan Naumann. I continued to coach the Glendale Gators during the summer months from 1972 through 1974. By ODU graduation, I had "learned my lessons well" and used them in the practicum of coaching the Glendale team and BOSC.

It was unclear what I would do for work in 1976. Then, a BOSC family (the Wood family – Mom Jane and female swimmer Dallas) paid for a graduate assistantship to continue graduate studies at ODU and continue coaching the BOSC. During this time, I had great assistant coaches named Beth Holmquist and Mark Bennett who helped to develop BOSC. Also, the Peninsula YMCA team, coached by a very good coach and friend named John Ryan, folded. Most of "the Peninsula" swimmers then joined BOSC which strengthened BOSC considerably.

This was an extremely stressful and tiring year. My son (*Ryan Allen Duncan*) was an infant with colic. I lived in Newport News, Virginia. I worked and attended graduate classes at ODU in Norfolk. Two mornings per week, I met swimmers' families in Newport News at 3:30 a.m. and drove swimmers to Norfolk for practice. I attended classes during the day, coached evenings, and stayed in the ODU library most nights until it closed around 10 p.m as I recall. I was working on a Thesis for my graduate degree.

The Thesis was concentrated on athletes' personalities and the study pool were athletes involved in all sports at ODU. Personality profiles on athletes were completed to answer these question(s):

1. Were certain personality types drawn to certain sports?

2. Were personality tendencies developed over the time that athletes were involved in their sport?

The conclusion was that certain personality types tended toward certain sports, a conclusion I have seen time and again as a competitive swimming coach. That is, swimmers might be very fast at racing swimming or even at practice; however, they eventually stop the sport of swimming if their personalities tend toward other activities. Likewise, I have seen swimmers stay with the sport of swimming, even when they are not "genetically" made for it.

Interestingly, wrestling and swimming were on opposite ends of the personality scale. As such, I leaned toward wrestling as my favorite sport for participation, but I have had considerable success as a swimming coach. That said, I still choose activities other than swimming for my personal enjoyment and fitness.

It was my hope with my graduate degree, that I would gain the ODU coaching position and continue to coach BOSC as my career—

at that time. BOSC won its first, and only, Virginia Age Group Championship in March of 1976. I failed to get the ODU college position that year. I also failed to be chosen by the Tritons Swim Team in Petersburg, Virginia.

So I attended the USA Junior National Championships (Gainesville, Florida) with swimmers that summer—and handed out resumes for coaching positions in hopes of being hired by (almost) any swim team.

I was hired by Coach Jim Montrella to start an AAU club in Vero Beach, Florida, as a division of the Indian River Community College Club program. This employment was a Godsend. It allowed time for me to recover, physically and mentally, from the stress of the previous year at ODU. The work hours were much less, the compensation was a good amount to live acceptably, and I had the opportunity to form a relationship with a Master Coach in Jim Montrella. Jim was not only a Master Coach, he (and his wife Bev) were outstanding people in terms of living values and working role models for me. My time in Vero Beach was only 10 months, but the positive influence they had on me has lasted a lifetime. Likewise, the Vero Beach swimmers and families were eager to learn. They made giant strides in that short time.

In May 1978, I was hired by the team for which I failed to get employment the previous year – Tritons of Petersburg. They fired the coach they had chosen and contacted me (again) to see if I was interested in returning to Virginia to coach. I was.

Twelve swimmers were training that summer. 78 came out in the fall. This team built a very good record of performance between 1978 and 1989. We started with assistant coaches Diane Cayce and Mark Kutz, both of whom eventually gained excellent recognition as high level coaches in their own right. Diane Cayce eventually coached 5 Olympians in various age-group programs, and Mark Kutz became a valuable assistant to Geoff Brown in the nationally recognized NOVA of Virginia team.

This program started as Tritons of Petersburg. It later became the Virginia Association for Competitive Swimming (VACS). This team's high achievements were: 2nd place at YMCA Nationals in 1983 and 3rd place at Short Course Women's USAS National Championships in 1989. Many swimmers qualified for National Championships and Olympic Trials in 1988, most senior swimmers graduating to College scholarships, and regular State Championships at the Age Group and Senior levels. Whitney Hedgepeth qualified for the 1988 USA Olympic Team out of this program.

I became divorced and remarried during these years. I married *Jeannie* and added my stepdaughter, *Julie*, to my family, which included my son Ryan. This was a (new) beginning on another level of life.

———

VACS merged with the Briarwood of Richmond Swim Team in April 1989. A main reason for the merger was to put the strongest two swim teams south of the James River and in Virginia together in the hopes that (together), a new aquatic center could be built in a central location between the two existing programs. It was thought the combination of swimmers would benefit from a dedicated aquatic center and consistent coaching for both teams. The name of the new team was Poseidon Swimming.

Briarwood had a better training facility than VACS but they had endured 6 head coaches over 8 years. VACS had experienced the same coach for 11 years. Me. The formation of Poseidon Swimming under my direction was considered a win-win circumstance. The name Poseidon was chosen as an elevation of the Triton name from earlier years.

The merger lasted for one year. The VACS Board of Directors changed shortly after the merger. The new VACS BOD, in a short-sighted decision, decided after the first year to return to its own program. I stayed with the new program called Poseidon.

Now Poseidon was a rather weak team after the failure of the merger. But by 1992, it was becoming the lead team in Virginia. By 1996, Poseidon was perennial state champion and placed 7th at the USAS Short Course Women's National Championships in that year. A 1996 graduate of Poseidon—Rada Owen—qualified for the 2000 USA Olympic Team. Poseidon had achieved the same success levels as VACS by 1996.

It was in 1996 that I came to the idea of a sports complex to mirror the USA Olympic Training Center—but on a local level. From my experiences at the Olympic Training Center in Colorado Springs, Colorado, it was evident (to me) that all athletes who were selected to train at the OTC were "raised in consciousness" from their interactions with each other and with coaches on the campus.

From a meeting hosted by the Richmond Sports Backers at offices of the Richmond Renaissance, I learned that most of the sports teams around Richmond had, with their respective teams' visions, to build their own individual training and competition facilities. My thought became that we could share economies of scale by working together in the formation of a sport(s) campus. All participating athletes and teams would benefit from interactions in a similar way to those athletes at the USA Olympic Training Center. All that was needed was a landowner with enough land and a vision for the idea…or so I thought.

A landowner was found in the Sowers family, which had been working in Richmond area real estate development for generations. The first of the Sowers family to have an interest was Buddy Sowers. Eventually Buddy's brother Mark became interested. Mark owned a more central location, and Buddy agreed. SportsQuest was born. I wrote an extensive business plan and began to promote it.

I also engaged in a nine-month fundraising curriculum at the University of Richmond. I organized a Board of Directors for a 501c3 non-profit business called SportsQuest, Inc. The SportsQuest BOD consisted of the leaders of the sports organizations, a lawyer, an accountant, a sports medicine professional and Jon Lugbill of Richmond Sports Backers. I applied for and gained legal status with the IRS.

The business plan had a simple vision, even though it was only about 20 pages long. The basic precepts of the plan were:

1. The landowner (Mark Sowers) would dedicate his land site (approximately 200 acres) to the complex.

2. Chesterfield County would pay to put infrastructure onto and into the land site in return for economic impact of events and some usage of the complex.

3. The infrastructure placed into and onto the complex would allow sports organizations to purchase and/or lease sites, and Mark Sowers to sell (or lease) sites to various sports organizations to build their facilities at reduced costs. It was considered that the facilities would be built to standards for high level competition and training. The campus was planned and drafted by HKS Architects, Inc., which had experience with sports development. Their Sports Development Department designed the campus at the Disney Wide World of Sports in Orlando, Florida.

4. SportsQuest, Inc., would raise funds (professionally) for the collective sports, much the same as collegiate athletic departments; that is, a fundraising professional and staff would be employed to fundraise for the collective group of sports organizations housed on the complex. SportsQuest, Inc., would also manage the common areas of the campus facilities.

Win! Win! Win!—Sowers! Chesterfield County! SportsQuest!

Once again, the underlying purpose of SportsQuest was to elevate consciousness for Sports in the Richmond, Virginia, demographic altogether. That is, all athletes regardless of their respective sports would benefit from their interactions with each other—similar to what was the case at the USA Olympic Training Center. *That said, my primary motivation was to create a stimulus that would elevate Poseidon swimmers' consciousness.*

A few significant people were instrumental to the progress of the SportsQuest movement:

- *Karen Kelley*, a Poseidon board member, strongly supported the concept. She encouraged support of the idea that my role at Poseidon should transition to a CEO role where I could administer the business responsibilities of SportsQuest while I coached in all Poseidon practice groups on a "visiting" basis— rather than to have specific responsibility for the senior level and the national ramifications along with it. Karen was extremely helpful and contributed a lot of personal time to the ideas of improving Poseidon as a business and SportsQuest as a movement.

- *Tracy Tynan* was employed by the Greater Richmond Partnership, the mission of which was to enhance economic development for metropolitan Richmond. Tracy opened doors to (a) HKS, Inc., an architectural firm which provided campus renderings and (b) Brailsford & Dunlavey, Inc., a company from Washington DC which was responsible for a DC/Baltimore bid for an Olympic Games. Tracy was also instrumental in using a Greater Richmond Partnership meeting room for SportQuest BOD meetings and Presentations.

- *Jon Lugbill*, CEO of Richmond Sports Backers, was active on the SportsQuest BOD and scheduled informational meetings with key business groups and individuals about the concept.

The SportsQuest effort continued for a total of 16 years. It was working well from 1996 until about 2002. *The Poseidon BOD decided, in the spring of 2000, not to support the concept—as of April 2000. This decision caused a significant difference between the BOD's vision and my vision for the team, resulting in my resigning from Poseidon—*

also in April 2000. Without my own team supporting the concept, SportsQuest went dormant by 2002 but picked back up again in 2007.

In 2007, leadership for the idea was different, and the business model was changed. Ultimately, despite best efforts and dedication of a core group of individuals, the idea of SportsQuest failed in 2012. I was selected to replace the "CEO" of the private company that also became SportsQuest, Inc. The company declared bankruptcy in 2012 due to unpaid debts.

All things considered, the disagreement between the BOD and myself demonstrates how a group of well-meaning volunteer parents can divert, or halt, the direction for a team and the leadership of a professional coach in a matter of weeks, or when there is a change in the structure of the BOD. It happened when a new VACS BOD pulled out of the original merger, and it happened in this instance with a change in officers on the Poseidon BOD. In both situations, I led the program's direction for 11 years—that is 22 years altogether for the two programs that were linked together.

Another element of consideration for club coaches is: While it feels great to have a supportive organization in your favor as you lead it, this can change without an insight into it, and it is the club coach who will experience the life change, not the volunteers. This book will help coaches be able to consider another pathway.

While this was disappointing to experience, it allowed me to move forward and better enabled me to handle the first year of my next venture.

———

The next endeavor in my coaching career was to purchase a swimming facility and a swim team. I did this in September 2003. This team became known as QUEST Swimming. I purchased the property and the team with partners. Eventually, I bought my partners out, and I now own the business.

The success of QUEST has been similar to VACS and Poseidon, but the journey has been somewhat different because our market is more competitive. A successful team (NOVA of Virginia) formed north of the James River in 1996 and dominates that portion of the competitive swimming market. Poseidon Swimming remains in existence and attracts a certain portion of the market south of the James River. A $14 MM swimming facility was built in Chesterfield County in 2012. It has been an attractive alternative to competitive swimmers in the market with an ideal facility and a team called SwimRVA. The former VACS team is merged with NOVA and is called NOVA-South.

Competitive swimming "south of the River," remains fragmented such that swimmers are divided amongst numerous teams. Together, it is largely recognized that the collective of those swimmers could benefit from one training/competitive system – but cooperation for the concept has yet to be realized.

Now – while QUEST has not won state championships, it has qualified swimmers through Olympic Trials during (almost) every Olympiad since 2004. But this team still focuses on "the middle of the bell curve" to develop swimmers to (at least) their next level of participation.

QUEST functions differently from most club programs. It is privately owned and operates differently from the standard. I have worked for non-profit swim teams throughout my career until QUEST. My relationships with Board of Directors members was always good – until it wasn't. And when it wasn't – there was a separation and it happened quickly.

This is what I learned from working with non-profit swim teams:

- The philosophy and the vision for the organization can

change abruptly when board members change.

- Most BOD members are great, well-meaning people; however, the operational paradigm is too scattered for seamless transitions from the standpoint of consistent forward vision as it relates to the club over time. Decision making on this basis is often flawed, and the flawed decision making can cause regression over the direction of a club.

- Most BODs (collectively) have a ceiling for what they think a swim coach should earn in compensation: that is, regardless of how well a coach is educated and qualified, how much a team grows, how well swimmers at all levels progress, how smoothly the administration works, and a vision for the future exists during the leadership of a coach, the board (typically) will not pay that coach beyond what "they think" the coach should earn. Typically, that is compared to what school teachers earn in the area. They may also tend to have whatever they earn themselves in their consciousness and they often seem to want a coach to make less than that ceiling.

- There is a constant argument about the level the program should achieve – and this can change at any moment in time when members want to act "politically" to change the direction of the team.

From my ownership of my property and my business I have learned:

- The work requires more time and effort to achieve ultimate power; that is, I can decide what I make based on affordability within the business. I can (and do) decide that I will make less when expenses are greater than revenues. That said, I have also made considerably more when revenues exceeded expenses.

- Living as a business owner is like living on a river. The flow of money is like the flow of the river. As long as you take care of the river (money), you can take from it, but you have to be careful to replace what you take. As long as the river (money) is healthy, the business can continue to grow and the owner can realize gains on several different levels.

- The team and the program can continue without "political" change.

- If I own my facility, I truly own the business. If I don't own my facility, the owners of facilities with which I contract for pool/dry land time own my program too. They are controlling partners in effect.

- Profitability and taxes are an interesting exercise. As the only member of my LLC, my personal taxes and the business taxes are blended. The business is shown in "Schedule C" within my personal tax returns. Most years, my tax returns have shown profits while I have always been challenged with cash flow in the business.

All things considered, if I would have purchased a swimming pool and owned my team from the start, knowing what I know now, greater results and experiences could have been achieved at ALL levels of competition.

Swimming pools can be purchased for the price of a typical mid-priced home. This will not be a good pool necessarily, but it can be made adequate for team operations. A new (25 yard, 6 lane) pool can also be built for about $500,000, including land. Again, that amount will not build a good pool, but it will build a pool that holds water and that is what is needed as a basic facility for success.

A pool would have cost much less when I was young. This would have allowed me to control my destiny for life, according to my abilities. I was always controlled, even when I did not know it. Some coaches, and people, are lucky in life. They seem to have good working circumstances altogether.

But most of us are not lucky. That is true for me for sure. Effort determines luck most often. Positive thinking and good use of one's abilities help a person to control their destiny.

I state this now for young, ambitious coaches. If you are willing to work more than the average person wants to work, you can make your way by owning your pool. I have known plenty of coaches who do not choose to own their facility because of the work that is required, but it has been good for me.

I retired from coaching in January 2019. The lead up in this book has been to show the path that my coaching career took and to emphasize that coaches can own their business. They can control their destiny if they want to. I understand, it is not for everybody. But I wish now that I had done so from the beginning. Therefore, I share this for those who do not know how or who fear the challenge. You can do it too!

Some general facts to help you further understand how I came to own my own club and facility:

1. I assumed a mortgage on an older pool in 2003 for $225,000. Since I assumed an existing loan, there was not a cash down-payment. The mortgage is paid in monthly installments. I had partners, but I didn't need them. All of the work was mine to do. Eventually, I bought them out to own it solely.

2. I refinanced this mortgage on two occasions to gain cash from equity on the property.

3. It was zoned residential, as it was a homeowners' association when the pool was constructed originally.

4. The pool was re-plastered in 2012.

5. The property was appraised for $468,000 in 2017.

6. The property was re-zoned in 2020 to C3 (commercial) to qualify to build a "teaching" pool and a building on the

property. This project is complete, and we had the Grand Opening on February 27, 2023.

7. It was appraised (with the project) at $2.62 MM, including renovations during 2020 – 2021.

Just like your swimmers, if you have the desire, you can control your own destiny, most of the time.

1 — A Way

From *Boys in the Boat* by Daniel James Brown, a statement by George Yeoman Pocock:

"It is hard to make that boat go as fast as you want to. The enemy, of course, is resistance of the water, as you have to displace the amount of water equal to the weight of men and equipment, but that very water is what supports you and that very enemy is your friend. So is life: the very problems you must overcome also support you and make you stronger in overcoming them."

Understand this: Being a good coach is not about having fast swimmers. Being *recognized* as a good coach is dependent on having fast swimmers. But honestly, fast swimmers can probably be fast with many coaches other than you, and slow swimmers will probably be slower than fast swimmers, regardless of you, even when you are trying your best to help them to be fast.

It is swimmers in the middle of the bell curve who benefit significantly from your coaching. It has been said generally, that a good coach makes about 2% of difference to an athlete. Now, that 2% could be the difference between a world record or not. I'm not sure if 2% is correct. In my experience, it is more or less depending on the circumstances. Of course, you might make some mistakes which reduce the average benefit to your athletes.

You might want to think of it as 2% per year and, for the club coach, that seems more accurate.

But, with that 2% difference, you may enable hundreds of swimmers who have average ability. You help them to reach their greatest potential. They, in turn, help your team by scoring when you did not expect it, or when they carry a relay when you would not have enough swimmers for the relay without them.

Keep in mind, these are most of the swimmers that you will coach in your lifetime. Be highly motivated to help them to become faster. They represent the large center of the bell curve.

At QUEST, we often say, and it is often said by others, that we have "a way of doing things." The way is stated simply in our motto which is: *We are dedicated to teaching the Art of Swimming and to perfecting the Game of Racing.* The objective in this chapter is to present the details related to that statement and our motto.

———

Human intelligence (generally) falls into two general and broad categories as it relates to swimming: creative intelligence and analytical intelligence. At QUEST, we are dedicated to teaching the Art of Swimming and to perfecting the Game of Racing. We have chosen this statement as our motto for operations because this is what we do. We teach the art of swimming and try to perfect the game of racing.

At QUEST, we like to think of swimming as an art and, therefore, teach and train with a mostly creative intelligence mindset. There are analytical elements like angles of entry, application of force, use of levers and other elements of physics which are not ignored, but not considered artistic. The swimmer applies almost every element of swimming with a sense of touch; that is, "feel for the water."

We refer to the Art of Swimming because we treat swimming as an art form. Water is the medium for movement. The swimmer needs to have that sense of touch, or feel, for the water. There are several elements of "feel for the water" that are relevant.

Obviously, the better a swimmer can feel the pressure of water on the hands and arms as they press progressively through strokes, the better the swimmer can apply appropriate force on the water and vice versa; that is, the better the water can receive the application of force, the better the movement.

There is also the movement of the body through the water. The swimmer feels the movement of water that surrounds the body and tries to reduce the resistance of the body's mass as it moves.

The feel for water surrounding feet and legs is unique. Propulsive force can be generated, but there is a high energy cost to the effort. Sometimes, kicking is simply to maintain a horizontal positioning on the water. The swimmer needs to feel for water pressure but it is also reasonable to apply appropriate force for efficiency. We like to think of using kicking to create something similar to gears in cars; that is, to enable faster movement as one intensifies kicking efforts.

A longer "vessel" is faster, and more efficient, than a shorter "vessel"; therefore, extension of the arms and hands to maximum length in stroke recovery is important to the overall art.

Vessel efficiency is most evident in kayaks, specifically kayak touring—not white water kayaking. I own a 13½-foot kayak which is wider for stability and a 19-foot kayak which is sleek for movement in the water. I lived on a reservoir and had a normal course from my house at one end of the reservoir to the other end of it. It took 2 hours to kayak in the shorter kayak and 1 hour 40 minutes in the longer kayak.

I do sometimes speak in analytical terms for those "engineering" types of minds. For them, terms such as angles of entry, use of leverage in the water, force application and body positions are important language terms; however, the swimmer still needs to be able <u>to feel</u> those elements while moving.

▬▬▬

At QUEST, we believe that coaches should be dedicated, and committed, to re-stating and re-explaining the same fundamentals daily and endlessly, because swimming for human beings is counter-intuitive. Stated further, that one's instincts for swimming are opposite from the movement actions that will make the swimmer more efficient. It is said by some that, of the human population, possibly 1% of it will swim efficiently if left to their instincts.

Take a drowning human, for example. The normal instinct to survive will be to:

1. Lift the head to keep it above water for breath.

2. Leverage the movement of the hands and arms downward to try to stay upright.

3. Kick the legs and feet in a vigorous way (possibly haphazardly) to stay up on the water.

4. All of this tends to happen vertically

This is the raw(est) version of human instinct.

To be efficient, swimmers should:

1. Lean the head backward or forward into the water, press the weight of the body toward the lungs, so as to help the body line become more horizontal—and with the head back or face down. If the face is pointed down and into the water, the swimmer should breathe to the side, or raise the head to a minimum lift.

2. Use arms to extend and lengthen the body line (on the recovering side of strokes) and press backward (on the pulling side of the stroke) to move the body horizontally

3. Move legs and feet (feeling the pressure of the water against legs and feet) only as much as is necessary to keep the legs on a plane with the hips.

4. All of this should happen in a horizontal line and with direction of movement

Note: A swimmer does not need to be perfectly still to float.

Floating is maintaining a horizontal position on the water with a minimum of movement of arms and legs, such that there is literally no fatigue resulting.

All of us who know how to swim accept this. However, we use our instincts regardless. If we are not taught, and unless it is reinforced to be efficient on a daily basis, we will return to our instincts; thus we will become more vertical and less efficient.

Further, we gain our greatest potential in physical power by generating movement from the core body.

On dry land, baseball players, tennis players, golfers, throwers, etc. ,anchor feet to the ground surface, gain a side stance (mostly), lead with the hip on the swinging side, and coordinate the arms/hands to the hips—and "let fly." If one starts the arm's movement before the hip moves, there is a significant loss of potential power. This relates to TIMING which is THE most important element of efficiency, and the most important element of the potential to gain power in movement.

The best example of this is when the soccer-style field goal kickers were first used in the NFL. Before that, kickers were mostly heavy lineman with great leg strength who used a straight-on kicking style.

Soccer-style kickers would come to the football at an angle and rotate the hips as they swung the leg to create a force in geometric progressions greater than the straight kicking form. Smaller soccer players were kicking the football significantly farther, with more accuracy than large lineman who had much greater strength.

This applies to freestyle and backstroke swimming as well. That is, if the hand moves to pull before the top hip moves, it will reduce the potential for power in the movement in geometric proportions.

For breaststroke and butterfly swimming, it is necessary to

have the hips in the right place at the right time for efficiency. The swimmer will realize more economy of effort in this way.

Finally, there is "feel for the water." This is most important to movement. The swimmer should feel the pressure of the water against one's hands and arms as they press in the opposite direction for movement. The movement of hands and arms should happen with progressive speed to keep the feel of the water pressure. Otherwise, water moving water occurs, which will inhibit the body's movement.

Breaststroke is considered to be different where "feel for the water" is concerned. The hands and arms move in a rather circular pattern, where it is important for the forearms and hands to move (almost) vertically below the elbows on the in-sweep – and the feet push backward and inward toward each other (from the buttocks) until the toes touch each other and point to form a horizontal body line.

Feel for the water is against the hands and arms as they circle outward, but the water actually surrounds them as they sweep inwardly. The feel for the water seems more like pressure rushing over both sides of arms and hands. Further, the speed of this movement should be extremely fast, such that the hand speed continues forward and pulls the body forward, using a transfer of momentum to the horizontal body line.

The weight of the head should also "lunge" forward and downward as the hands continue forward into the horizontal body line.

It is with ALL of this in mind that we refer to swimming as art when it comes to movement in water, or swimming. To summarize, the Art of Swimming is respective to:

- Body lines that are horizontal and long (from fingertips to toes), knowing that a longer vessel is faster (and more efficient) than a shorter vessel.

- Balance points (that surround the lungs) – press into these balance points during movement to elevate the hips to horizontal-ness.

- Timing – have hips in the right place at the right time such that movement can be generated from the core body.

Freestyle – from the front quadrant position (the recovering arm in front of the head and shoulders while the lengthening arm remains in place to form the longest line possible). A perfect line will have the following: 1) lead arm extended, 2) head in line with the spine, 3) hips "stacked" so that one is higher than the other, 4) weight pressed under the chest and arm pit (the balance point), and 5) legs on an even plane with the hips.

The Catch: 1) elbow higher than wrist, wrist higher than fingertips on the extended arm, 2) entering hand overhead at the catch; that is, in the front quadrant relationship, 3) head in line with spine, 4) weight pressed into balance point(s) surrounding the lungs, having the effect of keeping hips elevated and, 5) the legs in line with the hips.

The upper hip will simultaneously push forward and downward as the entering hand/arm lengthens to full length and the pulling arm presses rearward with progressive hand speed to gain maximum distance on the stroke.

Quadrants: <u>Front Quadrant</u> – from the shoulders forward, <u>Rear Quadrant</u> – from the shoulders backward, <u>Lower Quadrant</u> – the lower half of the body where an imaginary axis runs through the body's center, and <u>Upper Quadrant</u> – the upper half of the body above the axis.

Maintaining an ideally balanced line is important while turning for the breath: 1) the lead arm is fully extended, 2) the head has turned perfectly on its axis without lifting [one goggle remains in the water], 3) the swimmer is pressed into their balance point under the lungs such that the hips and legs remain elevated.

Hint: It may be helpful to think "lead with the hip" since human instinct is to pull first from the catch. If the pulling hand moves before the hip, power is significantly diminished. Eventually and ideally, the three movements occur simultaneously for perfect timing in the freestyle stroke.

This concept applies in all four strokes; that is, when the hips are in the right place at the right time, one can exert the greater potential for power while realizing the most economy of effort.

Note: Bernoulli's Principle – Fluid pressure is reduced whenever the speed of flow is increased. Hand speed on the in-sweep in breaststroke is critical to the amount and the speed of forward lift as the lift brings the body to breath. There are static Bernoulli's and dynamic Bernoulli's. Pertaining to flight, static is as in airplane wings and dynamic is as in helicopter blades where the blade travels at alternating speeds on one side of the circle versus the other side. Breaststroke is this way as hand speed moves from slower to faster from the out sweep to the in sweep and forward.

Timing – All of breaststroke mechanics should occur with ideal timing; that is, the hips should be at their highest point when the arms are extended to their longest length. This will allow the core body to drive downward and forward for maximum upper body power while the feet recover naturally; that is, without the need to pull the feet up toward the buttocks.

<u>Transfer of Momentum</u> – Hand speed must continue to accelerate forward (in breaststroke) such that the body mass follows the hands toward a long and horizontal line for ideal forward movement.

There are "stroke flaws" which should be corrected when the

coach sees them.

- The elbow should be on a higher plane than the wrist, and the wrist should be on a higher plane than the fingertips.

- The head should be in line with the spine.

- Breath should happen low to the water in freestyle and butterfly.

- Breath should happen rhythmically in backstroke.

- Breath should happen as the in-sweep brings the head to air in breaststroke.

These are things that can be corrected easily by stating the correction (usually).

The Art of Swimming refers to total body movement in water – and we stress those elements daily. We attend to it in warm ups and swim downs, pure recovery swims, etc. But it is constant re-enforcement to overcome human instinct, which is to leverage with the arms/hands and to lift the head to breathe.

Another kayak analogy is appropriate regarding swimming body movement. Most people propel a kayak by pulling backward on the oar with their arms. To increase power in geometric proportions, one should place the oar into the water—then use the opposite hip and the opposite arm to push on the opposite side of the oar forward, while pulling simultaneously on the section of the oar in the water. The water side of the oar gains purchase on the water, but power is gained from pushing on the other side of the oar. Again, the longer and more streamlined the skull of the kayak, the kayak will gain more distance with each stroke of the oar.

As it pertains to freestyle, imagine that a rod is connected from the topside hip to the recovering arm – and the hip pushes the rod and the recovering arm simultaneously with the movement of the pulling arm. Power gains in geometric proportions will be realized on each stroke. This happens best when the recovering arm reaches the front quadrant position.

One of the best examples of this timing was Janet Evans, a world record holder in all freestyle distances from 400 meters to 1500 meters. Janet's swimming career culminated at the 1988 Olympics. Many coaches were critical of her "round house" recovery style; however, her hip on the recovery side was perfectly timed to her arm as she would "throw" it altogether with force. The pulling arm was timed to the recovery movement and her feel for the water was excellent. Janet was quite small compared to her competition, although her body was very sleek and moved exceptionally well in the water. Janet also had tremendous aerobic capacity and will to win.

She split 2:02 – 2:01 to go 4:03 for 400 meters at the 1988 Olympics—and to win over East Germans who were on each side of her in the lanes—in World Record time. All of the swimmers were close at 200 meters, but Janet negative split while the East Germans were at least 2 seconds slower on the last 200 meters of the race. Janet played *the game of racing* to perfection and seemed to be joyful in it.

We want to imprint, as much as possible, the nervous system to perform according to the knowledge that lends itself to the art. Thus, swimmers can be as fast as possible with the greatest economy of effort possible.

And The Game of Racing!

To watch 8 & under swimmers race is purely joyful, once they know how to swim, that is.

Note: It is not joyful to watch children who are not ready to race – race. They are not joyful when hanging on lane lines and fearful of getting to the other end of the pool – or not.

But – when they are ready – they are most joyful in the activity of racing. When they complete the race, they typically go to their parents/family to hear that the effort was good, then run off to play. This is a natural joy that we want to keep in competitive swimmers. This is why we refer to the "game of racing." It is a way of play. To lose the innocence and joy of racing can cause one to be on a "slippery slope" as it relates to the joy of the experience.

Thus, the Game of Racing is a constant reminder that it is fun to race. As swimmers mature there are many factors that can "chip away" at the FUN of racing. While there is a process of development which may hide the fact at times, we should all do our best to keep racing fun and the fun of racing in our consciousness.

I believe that it is better to coach competitive swimmers to race

with their competitors rather than to race *against* their competitors. This indicates a responsibility to others—to give one's best effort— and tends to relieve some of the pressure of losing to an opponent. The will to win should be at the essence of a person, but it is not to defeat the other person. It is to give respect to the other person by one's highest possible level of performance. It is to give honor to the opponent and to be honored by the opponent to have a great RACE.

To give less than one's best effort is to dishonor the competition.

One swimmer who exemplified the game of racing, and the joy of it, was named Jeff Utsch. Jeff liked distance races the most. He seemed to enjoy his races every time I watched him race. He would normally swim to the speed of the person out front in the race. He did not like to lead from the start when competing with equals. He liked to play the game of coming from even or behind to win. It was rather like he used the energy of the competition to energize himself. He would choose his time to overtake the competition and eventually race for the win. He liked to better his times, but he liked winning his races more than he liked bettering his times. His times continued to get faster throughout high school, but they did so from racing faster levels of competition. Jeff was one of the purest examples of the "game of racing" that I recall from my years of coaching.

Different swimmers like to race differently. Some like to lead from the beginning. Some like to "swim their own race" according to a strategy they have planned. Some will analyze their competition before and/or right up until the race. Some like to use psychological tricks in a ready room, behind the starting blocks and even on the starting blocks and some like to relax themselves with music and such. Whatever the personal approach to racing, it should be fun to race and it should be done with respect for the competition. Good races are important to everyone's development toward becoming the best one can be.

That said, we have a formula for speed. It is:
Speed = Stroke Length x Stroke Rate (plus "the will to win")

We also use the (Dudley) axiom that "90% of races are won in the last 15% of the race." This is not according to a scientific study. It is something that I observed to be largely true in my early career and I have made the statement ever since. Regardless if it is perfectly true, or not, it most often happens that when swimmers are in close races with equals, to have greater energy than your opponent at the end of the race tends to be an advantage in winning the race.

This first came to my notice when I took the team I was coaching (Tritons of Petersburg) to a meet at the Startlit Aquatic Center in Northern Virginia. This was about 1980. A team called Foxcatcher was attending the meet. They were coached at the time by George Haines, a Hall of Fame coach who also founded and coached a team called Santa Clara Swim Club for most of his career and won 43 National Championships while coaching there.

Well – I noticed during the 2½ days of competition that Foxcatcher swimmers were regularly in races to win heats and many of them were in the faster heats. The element that stood out in these races was that the Foxcatcher swimmers seemed to be strategizing to win races at the end of the races—or they had that physical capability. I'm not sure if, in truth, those swimmers were strategizing to win races on the closing laps or not. It seemed that way as I observed their racing during the weekend.

It was following that weekend that I first made the statement to my team that 90% of races are won in the last 15% 0f the race. And – I began to coach accordingly.

Other than the art of swimming, training must provide a basis for cardiovascular and muscular endurance, and the mind must understand race strategies that will allow for a winning result.

We use another slogan that I learned from a good friend and coaching colleague named Terry Laughlin, founder of the teaching company called Total Immersion; that is: No Brain No Gain. We practice race strategies such that swimmers understand "build points" during races to achieve their best (winning) results.

There will be a chapter on this later in the book, but it is relevant for the reader to know it is understood that efficiency, in and of itself, is not enough to be accomplished as a competitive swimmer. Training is needed to be ready to win races against one's equals. Training is needed to race through the duration of multiple day meets with equals.

I understand this; however, it is the mind first which puts training into measurable action plans for training.

2 — Team Consciousness

"One finger can't lift a pebble" – a Hopi proverb.

Consciousness is defined as follows:

- "The fact of awareness by the mind of itself and the world"

- "Of the mind or thought directly perceptible and of control of the person concerned"

- "Of an action or feeling deliberate and intentional"

Team Consciousness is when the collective minds relate according to things that are understood—and—<u>THE TEAM</u> is aware of the elements that are required to achieve "the way" the team wants to represent itself.

The normal time that it takes to develop a change in team consciousness is about three years. My experience has been that the first stage is to help swimmers to understand the "true" nature of competition; that is, to come together to help each other become more competitive and to learn the basic skills (or fundamentals) of swimming (and racing).

The second stage has been to advance, according to what is required, to achieve a level of competition that is beyond perceived natural capabilities. Examples of this are to help swimmers to believe that they can reach levels beyond where they are:

- to become an A swimmer from B level,

- to be a state champion,

- to achieve a national qualifying time,

- to be a national champion,

- to make Olympic Trials,

- to make the Olympic team, or

- to medal at the Olympic Games.

Of course, the numbers of swimmers that achieve levels approaching Olympic participation are larger than the number who make the Olympic Team – and so – they are collectively important to each other.

The small number that achieve at the highest levels in the sport "pull" the groups toward that by their great achievement—as a possibility. The swimmers that are team members in the same process are achieving according to their potential and at levels that are considered to be greater than their natural abilities.

Interestingly, changes in consciousness do not happen as swimmers actually achieve higher levels of performance. They happen as the team accepts "the standards" of preparation for performance. In other words, achievement usually follows preparation.

The standards at a basic level have to do with discipline. This takes place over four stages:

1. Discipline might be imposed at an introductory stage, but it turns into self-discipline eventually, when swimmers accept the value of discipline for themselves and others.

   For example: For most of my memory, I have started every group on every team from a real start; that is, "Take your mark," and "GO!" It is no joke. All swimmers are expected to be on time and start the practice with the best start they can do. It is important to me that every swimmer take the start seriously. This way, all group members start together, perform the start well and realize that —to start practice—this is expected. There was a real possibility that if one did a poor effort on the start or was not on time, they would not practice that day. In early team development stages, there was always some resistance to this but later it was

*accepted as "the way we start" and swimmers took advantage of
the opportunity to improve their starting form (for the most part).*

2. The second stage is when the collective team is using learned
    skills that define their performances; that is, their skills are
    recognizable to others as they perform them.

3. The third stage has to do with training the physiology, such
    that learned skills can be used with speed over distance and
    time. And, this element needs to be able to happen over days
    of time.

4. The last stage is for the swimmers to have confidence that
    they can compete to win with their equals (or people that
    have achieved higher performance levels).

Assuming that each of these stages in raising consciousness takes
about 3 years, it will take between nine to 12 years to develop the
highest stage of consciousness, depending on the beginning point.
This means that all of the team (swimmers, coaches, families, and
the support of the community) accept and promote the sources of
continuity (for development) that run through the TEAM.

I have seen and heard of coaches who accelerate the process of
change by imposing discipline and demanding changes in behaviors
quickly, but they tend to be short-lived as teams. Some might advance
performance with imposed discipline, but the majority might be
sacrificed in that paradigm. I have also seen and heard of situations
where key people are un-accepting of change such that they inhibit
the advancement of teams.

Many things can happen and do happen. Ironically, the higher
the expected levels of team consciousness, the more vulnerable the
TEAM is to a reversal and/or regression in team consciousness.

The moral of this story is to be patient. Allow time for people to
change. Figure in:

1. Time to transition from imposed discipline to self-discipline

2. A year to imprint skill development into nervous systems

3. A year to elevate training capabilities while using imprinted skills

4. Experience the confidence that comes in competing with equals and the expectation to win races

Most groups work according to, and within, a bell curve. To be specific, every group consists of swimmers who advance quickly, swimmers that are in between the quick accelerators and swimmers who are slower to advance. This is true for performance but it is also true as it relates to consciousness.

If we imagine a line that intersects the middle of the bell curve, our mission is to move the mid-line toward greater excellence.

An example would be to move a Team from a consciousness for competing at a State level to one that expects to compete at a National level. The idea is to move the middle line. Of course certain individuals might move more quickly, but the key is the middle. Does their consciousness change? The process is relatively slow by its nature. In fact, it can be like watching the grass grow.

It happens without your specific awareness of seeing it, but at some point in time you realize that it has grown. Consciousness cannot be easily seen to change, but at some point you realize that it is different. The line has moved and the normal expectation(s) for the collective Team are elevated.

Changing consciousness means that the coach is working to advance the mental approach of the Team. Notice that in the definition of consciousness there is reference to the mind, an action that is deliberate—and intentional.

Communication is a key mechanism for advancement of

consciousness. And – it is wise to communicate in as many forms as possible to affect as much of the team as possible; that is, communicate with swimmers, families, coaches, and community. They are collectively integral to team consciousness. Some important elements to Team Consciousness are:

- Having a handbook with a clearly defined Philosophy, Vision, Mission, Values, Goals, Objectives, Policies and Procedures, and Definitions (for training groups, etc.)

- A Website updated with "the workings" of the Team. This should include team records, meet schedules showing all levels of competition, a process leading toward desired levels of participation and competition, team history and direction, practice groups (with descriptions), registration methods, performance results, achievements of swimmers and coaches, and more

- Social media postings where events and results are posted for the community

- Newsletters and Bulletin Board(s) that highlight important achievements and events

- White Board communications

- Record Boards (updated)

- Coaches meetings with swimmers (group and individual) and parents

- Goal Setting sessions, reinforcement, and feedback

- Qualifying Standards

The list of items to impact the fact of awareness by the mind of itself and the TEAM is as long as people are creative in communicating. As we approach 2024 the opportunities seem endless compared to what opportunities existed when I started coaching in 1968.

As time passes, and levels of performance are raised, it is the norm that the process, or "the quest" to higher levels changes as Team Consciousness changes.

For example: when swimmers are at beginning stages of development, it is not unusual for their performance achievements (dropping times and winning heats) to happen in consecutive swim meets. However, as swimmers advance and are more experienced, they get closer and closer to their "trained" potential.

This happens according to other changes as well such as advancing age, growth and maturity (physically and mentally), and movement skills/racing strategies become more of who they are. These circumstances, or this circumstance, can demonstrate that more time is needed to surpass the best performance(s) from the past.

When coaches, swimmers, and parents reach greater maturity, or higher consciousness, they understand that performance(s) which are less than the lifetime best are positive performances toward a desired end, rather than negatives away from the desired end. This allowance for training and adaptation time is significant.

It is also very important to re-emphasize here that no one is "accepting" lower performance as an end, but rather "understanding" that time, training process, meets, and efforts toward a positive action plan are reasonable experiences to perform above natural potential. This is an element of changing team consciousness as more individual swimmers reach toward higher success.

An example of developmental interaction among swimmers might be: Swimmer A – "How did you do?" Swimmer B – "I added time. It was horrible."

An example of higher consciousness interaction among swimmers in the same circumstance might be: Swimmer A – "How did you do?" Swimmer B – "I split my race as I planned and my time was better than at this time last season/year. I really pushed the race. I'm on track for what I want to do at the end of the season."

The race is the same, but the consciousness in the second interaction is elevated. When this happens such that coaches, swimmers and parents (collectively) have understanding, then team consciousness is elevated.

When understanding passes throughout the team, group to group and year to year, that is when the team is ready for development to the next level of consciousness.

Some teams continue to place swimmers at the highest levels year after year and generation after generation. This shows that leadership in the team is at a high level and that there is continuance according to standards that are high, and process that is understood and accepted.

Competition happens best when people are working together and WITH each other. Competition that happens AGAINST tends to be negative. Against—lends itself to ego, jealousies, perceptions of unfairness and feelings of "better than" or "less than," neither of which is actually true; that is, both are perceptions.

With—tends to be positive; that is, "We are all in this together, and we can help each other by trying our best at all times." This is true, not only within teams, but within sports in general. When it is understood that participants within a given sport are competing with each other to elevate each other's performance levels, it takes out negative feelings toward each other, but it also raises the importance of giving a BEST effort when others depend on other athletes for their individual performances.

There is a state of mind in Japanese samurai swordsmanship called "*satori*." It is also a feeling that exists after victory, because victory typically meant that one samurai lived and the other died in the fight. It is a feeling of elation and sadness at once, such that celebration of victory is within rather than outward—and showing "happiness" in the suffering of the competitor, or of the onlookers, (possibly family) is inappropriate.

There is also a quality in the competition called "*mushin*" which is to be altogether in the moment, such that skills are performed perfectly and instinctively (without thought). It means that training has happened well enough for the sword to be one with the samurai.

There was a television program I liked called "Hitsville." The program documents the story of Motown music and the development of the artists that became recognized as Motown artists. Gordon Berry was the seed for the development, and others such as Smokey Robinson, the Temptations, The Supremes, The Four Tops, et al., were recognized as Motown musicians and vocalists. During the documentary, it was spoken of the intense competition to be better in performance than each other. However, it was also noted that the competition was "with" each other, and that they loved each other more as Motown became more famous.

It was stated along with this, that competition without the love for each other, would turn to expression of egos, jealousies, and generally diminishing behavior that would NOT have tended toward the success that was experienced with Motown. This is an example of healthy TEAM consciousness.

This is an element of consciousness that nurtures long-lastingness. Nobody wants to lose. Everybody wants to win.

It is true that negative emotions can motivate winning efforts sometimes, but negative emotions will tend to flip performance in circumstances, whereas positive thinking will win over time.

———

We often see differences in how athletes celebrate victory. In swimming, it is not unusual to observe a winning competitor who throws fists into the water and/or elevates themselves above others by sitting on a lane line—to show dominance possibly.

Also, we often see competitors hug each other after a good race. The first is (probably) competing against and the second is (probably) competing with.

The results are the same, but the first might be causing the other competitors to feel "less than," while the second shows an appreciation to the other competitors.

At any given time, results can be turned when one is making others feel "less than," but this is not the case when competing with others.

These are consciousness matters.

There are physical adaptations as swimmers get faster and expect to be faster. These items happen as a matter of course, but can impact consciousness positively:

- The average intervals for send-offs get faster

- The challenge intervals get faster

- Times on repetitions get faster

- Faster times are achieved with lower stroke counts, more efficiency, lower heart rates, easier breath

- There is an ability to swim longer distances more comfortably

- Recovery happens with shorter rest

- Recovery is not needed as often

- One can swim fast after dry land or one can accomplish dry land well after swimming

- Resting heart rates are lower

- The swimmer can swim at higher stroke rates over distance and time without losing distance per stroke

- Swimmers finish repetitions better

- Swimmers turn faster

- Underwater skills improve

- Racing during practice becomes more intense

When all of these (type) elements are happening for most of the swimmers together, team consciousness has changed and team performance will be at a higher level of achievement.

This understanding is key for coaches. The coach needs to challenge swimmers with these elements and help athletes to believe that they can accomplish those challenges. The coach needs to recognize the need to be gradual and realistic when assigning the challenges, but the coach also needs to understand and help athletes to understand that failure to accomplish the challenge is a positive attempt. The athlete has to attempt challenges in order to succeed at them, even if they fail at the moment. That might mean failure for a time, but it will mean eventual success as the majority understand what is necessary to succeed.

This concept of failure as a natural occurrence when seeking success is a little "tricky," but it is a fact of developing a good team consciousness.

Angela Duckworth, in her book *Grit: The Power of Passion and Perseverance*, demonstrates, through examples in chapter after chapter, how this idea is true. The tricky element is that young people may be experiencing failure at its beginning. Their maturity may not be developed and sophisticated enough to have it in perspective.

Understand, it is unwise to set up circumstances for failure so regularly that it becomes the expectation rather than success. And know that the coach is responsible to put failure in perspective, and raise athletes up out of it when they are frustrated by it. The coach also needs to know that it is a step to success, so they do not get frustrated when expectations are for success, but the expectations are met with failure. It may be that the day is just not right. Return to previous practice items that will guide athletes toward the desired results until they are ready to achieve them.

———

Altogether it is important to understand that (at least) a decade of time might be dedicated to the development of a good team consciousness. This reality is very important for coaches to know and lead with patience to establish, for parents of swimmers to know (especially those who seek Board of Directors positions) and ultimately for athletes.

Athletes will be more aware at a deeper level when they become adults. Parents need to come to understand it—and to understand what they are de-mantling when they decide to "change the team." Coaches need to lead the process and recognize changes in consciousness to seek the next levels.

There are geographic areas within the United States that possess higher consciousness by the nature of how competitive swimming has developed over time. California, Florida, Texas, and Northern Virginia are a few examples of this. Therefore, more Olympians and other world class swimmers come from such places. Such areas of dominance have become less the case as more coaches have become educated and swimming has spread as a sport of choice, but do still exist.

Different countries have different systems for developing athletes. Certain body types tend to excel more quickly and naturally. In the United States, swimmers compete upward largely on the basis of natural selection; that is, we have hundreds of thousands of swimmers that start in the sport in hundreds of neighborhoods,

YMCAs, local recreational pools, schools, etc. It is rather like one collective tank of swimmers that compete until some reach the highest levels in the sport based on their physical stature, their desire, their coaching, their family support, their team consciousness, their community support, etc.

China is a country that is progressing quickly in world class competitive swimming, but they use a specific selection process for swimming athletes, and athletes in general. China collects swimmers from their geographic provinces who meet specific criteria, according to the understanding of "officials," needed to be competitive on a world class level. Their athletes are measured according to predicted height, gliding ability of their body type, reaction time, speed of underwater dolphin kicking, hand size, foot size, body weight, body density—and times in specific events, etc. The measurements are shown together on a spreadsheet. If swimmers qualify according to their measurements, then they are selected to train toward becoming world class competitive swimmers. Should swimmers fail to be competitive on a world class level, they are dropped from the training site and returned home. When selected, they train full time (often without school obligations) until they either remove themselves, or are removed by officials from training and competing.

As an example of differing consciousness between the USA and China, on my second experience coaching in China, it began with a competition of swimmers. In this competition there was a boy who demonstrated significantly superior speed and technical capabilities in all of his events. His height was about 5'9" and his predicted height did not meet the minimum standard for swimmers in his events. The leader of the "training camp" stated to the participating coaches that she would drop him from the camp due to his lower predicted height. While discussing the matter with the leader on behalf of the swimmer, she said to me: *(paraphrase)* "*In America, you have survival of the fittest with all of your pools and developing swimmers. It is different in China. If I take this boy into this group of developing swimmers, I will lose my position as leader because he does not meet the predicted height standard, and "he will be eliminated anyway."*

Altogether, one can see that consciousness develops according to a given swimmer's circumstance. It can also be understood that consciousness is an important element of development in sport.

Consciousness is of the mind; that is, it is unseen as a direct force within an individual – yet real and observable in behaviors of the individual.

Team consciousness is the same except it is relating to a collective mentality which aims at a perceived direction. That direction is nurtured by leaders who share the consciousness and who are dedicated to directing behaviors and actions of team members toward it.

For teams that I have led, those consciousness elements have been:

- To compete with noticeable, recognizable swimming technique

- To have <u>all</u> of the fitness needed for <u>all</u> competitive circumstances

- Enthusiasm for competition

- Team-ness

- Discipline (self and team) in training and competition

- An understanding that we compete with others, not against others

- The importance of <u>uniformity</u>

- An understanding of the relationship between racing and goals

This is always a work in progress. No teams (actually) reach a perfect and full team consciousness. It is ever changing according to changes in the individuals who are team members.

All are in a continuum of consciousness that is headed toward the decided elements of consciousness. It can be observed in its development, especially by those outside of the team, if they are observed regularly. But for coaches and leaders, it is a bit like watching grass grow.

Coaches and leaders should always live according to the consciousness elements that are desired. This is the beginning and the source of continuity for team consciousness over time.

3 — The Backbone

For most of my career, I have attended Coaching Clinics and/or Conferences where presentations focused on athletes who perform well in world class meets, or coaches' stories about the development of those athletes.

For the most part, these presentations held little relevance for me and the athletes that I was coaching, nor the team development for teams that I coached. There was occasionally valuable insight from social interactions at these events, but the actual information from the events was rarely useful.

This is not to advocate against such events, nor the associations that schedule such presentations. It is great to belong to associations and to participate with associations and colleagues in the profession. I advocate for attendance and participation.

However, all levels of swimming (summer league, YMCA, club, high school, collegiate, and professional) are different and should have different physiological and mental approaches to training and clinics about training. Of course, this seems obvious.

There is a constant and continual debate within competitive swimming about "how much" or "how little" yardage, "how much" or "how little" speed emphasis, "how much" or "how little" strength training, etc.

This debate is confusing, but it is even more confusing for developing club coaches who are working through the various levels of the profession, as assistant coaches or head coaches, within the variety of levels. It can be maddening to live in the middle of this debate, while trying to do your best for a team of swimmers who are in need of some specificity, which can be completely altered from their needs by this debate.

This book is written from the perspective of a USA-S Club coach, and this is integral to one of the reasons for me to undertake its writing. Different levels have different needs for training.

So I offer the following:

1. Summer League – Participants at this level should know how to swim. They should learn through lesson programs rather than on the swim team. This level should emphasize technique development in the four competitive strokes, individual medley, starts, and turns. This is the case because most swimmers are beginning to compete, or compete only during summer months for their neighborhood teams. The other element of training should be speed related because they typically swim 25-, 50-, or 100-yard distances in meets, including their championships. Their need for endurance can be realized during the course of developing technical elements – and racing or timing them. The goal should be for coaches to reinforce the need for using the technical elements during racing efforts. Repetitions in practice should be 100 yards and less to maintain good order and traffic flow in the practice, to prevent overwhelming new swimmers with excessive distance of repetitions, to allow concentration on skills and/or speed, and to keep this introductory level motivating to swimmers.

   Most often, summer league coaches are high school or college-aged people who have been relatively successful at year-round swimming. Oftentimes, they have trained at a senior club level and/or college level, where they have experienced endurance training combined with attention to speed training. It is not unusual for them to take these training elements into the summer league team circumstance, which is inappropriate for this level of swimmers. Many eventual coaches start at this level. It would be great for associations to offer classes to new coaches at beginning levels, or to regionalize clinics for those coaches.

2. YMCA – When I coached in the YMCA system, the YMCA had a stated philosophy for competition and specific to competitive swimming. It said: "Everybody Swims, Everybody Wins." However, there is a dichotomy in YMCA swimming:

   • YMCA teams which compete only in YMCA league meets

   • YMCA teams which also compete in USAS meets and aim to be competitive on higher levels of participation

   Those YMCA programs that wish to compete at higher levels often come into conflict with YMCA philosophy. Typically, this conflict leads to one of two circumstances.

   • The program is forced to reduce its commitment to competitive results in USAS meets, or

   • They leave the YMCA association.

   The rules of competition limit the number of events to 3, whether in dual meets, or the YMCA National Championships. Most swimmers compete at distances shorter than 200 yards. Swimmers who compete in longer distances are typically year-round and/or they compete in USAS as well as YMCA. Due to the limited number of events and the varied levels of individual swimmer development, the emphasis for most YMCA programs should also be on technical development, speed, and some attention to endurance. Endurance should be a matter of some cyclical approach, depending on the makeup of the training groups. There are a few exceptions to this thought process. For example, the Sarasota YMCA Sharks, and a few others, have been successful doing both but it is more often the case that there is a conflict with YMCA philosophy and USA-S development.

3. USA-S Club – This level is at the core of USA Swimming. Some would say it is *the backbone* of USA Swimming. It is through clubs, which exist nationwide, that most swimmers develop to national and international levels of competition.

That said, it is also the level at which most swimmers do not reach national and international levels.

This is where most swimmers fully develop competitive swimming skills, transitioning from skill development to training their physiology, and reaching their individual potential for competition. This is a brief description concerning USA-S Club Swimming here because there is more to discuss concerning USA Club Swimming.

4. High School – This is a very competitive level of swimming. High School is a time in human development when we are deep in search of two elements of maturity:

   • Social development – through a process of finding where and/or with whom we belong specific to groups

   • Independence or Self-Reliance – Thus, the often stated: "You don't have to tell me that!" or "I can think for myself, I don't need you to!" These types of statements from teenagers are indicative of a transition to adulthood and the need to be independent as adults.

   Therefore, to compete before peers is a high priority, especially if it leads to perceived approval or it shows self-reliance.

   That said, high school swimming also limits the number of swims in which one can race, the training time, and the championship circumstance. Given that, a good case can be made for skill development and high intensity, race specific training for high school teams. Teams are normally mixed with new swimmers, those who have summer league experience, those who have YMCA experience, and those who are swimming on USA Clubs in combination with their High School Teams. This creates a conundrum for the coach. Planning and organization are critical for optimum results for individuals as well as teams.

5. College – Similar limitations on meet events and training time exist in college swimming. Most college training programs focus time on an aerobic phase of training, usually culminating with a Christmas travel trip. However, it is sensible for colleges to train more high intensity and race specific training. Strength training is prioritized now because athletes have mostly completed their growth stages; therefore, their bodies are ready for strength training.

6. Professional – These are post collegiate, adult athletes that have reached the highest levels of competition at national/international levels. Their training is full time, race and physiology specific. Strength training can be intense at this level due to the fact that these swimmers are adults.

———

There are many debates surrounding club swimming. It is at this level that the debate over training volume versus training intensity persists – without clear answers for most coaches. Is there the right amount of yardage? Is speed sacrificed when more yardage is given? How much endurance is needed? The list goes on, but the questions all surround the idea of quality versus quantity.

There have been many changes which have lent themselves to interesting experimentations and thoughts on these matters since the 1960's.

1960's: When I started swimming in 1959, we did not wear goggles. They had yet to be developed for competitive training and racing. We practiced until our eyes were burning too badly.

Goggles use started about the late-1960's; therefore, training yardage/mileage began to increase as swimmers could train for longer time frames with goggles to protect eyes from "chlorine burn." As swimmers became able to train longer, and more specifically, they became faster as well.

1970's: The East German women burst into world class competition and were dominating in the early to mid-1970's. Their strength appeared exceptional; therefore, American coaches began to concentrate on dry land exercises for strength. Lowering body weight became an emphasis, especially for female swimmers. American coaches attended to these factors (almost) obsessively to be competitive with East Germany (mostly). As it turned out, the East Germans were using steroids and experienced enhanced performance on that basis.

Dry land exercise has had a continuing positive influence on training while body weight has, thankfully, reduced in importance as emphasis on body weight was a negative factor to the mental game for many female athletes. Still, yardage/mileage amounts continued to increase through the late '70's, reaching 20,000 yards in a day for some world class swimmers and others who participated in programs that focused on national and international competition .

1980's: During the late '70's and the early 1980's, racing suits and faster pools were being developed, which improved performances significantly. There were Belgrade suits, "paper" suits, and eventually the Technical Suits swimmers wear today. There were pools built and lane lines improved to reduce turbulence, while increased depth of water for racing reduced turbulence from pool floors. Overflow gutters reduced wall turbulence. Swimming times dropped significantly with these developments.

1990's: USA Swimming became its own governing body and moved out of the Amateur Athletic Union (AAU), moving to its home in Colorado Springs, Colorado, in about 1988. "Scientific" information began to be distributed from the Office of (Swimming) Science for USA-S. The American Swim Coaches Association (ASCA) also enhanced their mission of educating coaches during the late 1980's. This began the debate over quantity and quality amongst scientists, coaches, and athletes. It continues even now, and I suspect it will in the future. Education of coaches has been an equalizer for performance across the USA, and also around the world. When I started coaching, very few swim coaches were specifically educated and there were a few "hot spots" of swimmers. Today, due to widespread education of coaches from USA-S, the International Swim Coaches Association (ISCA), ASCA, and the World Swim Coaches Association (WSCA), the United States and the world are much more competitive, generally.

Note: As stated at the beginning of this chapter, there are numerous swimming levels and there is likely a good answer to the quantity/quality question for most of them, except the USA-S Club level. One objective for this book is to offer some enlightenment on the question for Club coaches specifically.

2000: The early part of the 21st Century was focused on Technical Swimsuits and performance times. Swimmers began to reach competitive performance times which were practically as enhanced as those for swimmers who were administered steroids during the late '70's and the 80's. Suits were more buoyant, full bodied, hydro-dynamic, and capable of better performance with less training. The question of more or less swimming in training was exacerbated. Alas, this performance enhancement was also controlled; therefore, back to the question of quantity and quality.

2010 – 2020: Most of the improvements in competitive swimming during this decade have come from professional swimming. There has been more sophisticated attention to dry land and the promotion of competitive swimming, such that better athletes are drawn to the sport—and stay in the sport in post college years.

Note: Professional swimmers have changed the performance horizons for Club coaches. It is the exception that high school swimmers can make Olympic Teams or World Championship Teams now. Some do make it, mostly specific to female swimmers, but the largest participation of those teams comes from collegiate or professional swimming programs.

I offer this brief historical perspective in the sport to show how the debate of quality/quantity developed and the factors that have been part and parcel to the question. Some developments have been illusions to the realities faced by Club coaches in preparing swimmers for their next level, or not.

But for Club coaches, the question has to consider the challenges of club swimmers who participate on several different levels in different multi-day meet formats over successive weeks—or even greater than a month of time.

Clearly, individual athletes have achieved various successes with different training emphases.

The first consideration regarding these elements is to define the responsibilities of a USA-S Club coach:

1. To establish a good foundation of fundamentals for swimmers; that is, regarding swimming technique, training, "the mental game," and dry land exercises.

2. To guide swimmers toward a higher potential for performance levels.

3. To prepare swimmers for what follows Club swimming, whether that be college club swimming, NCAA swimming, Masters swimming, Professional swimming – or – maybe USA-S Club swimming will be the end for some.

4. To have the skills for ideal safety and/or the use of swimming as a lifetime exercise for fitness.

The source of continuity among the responsibilities of a Club coach is that the coach is mostly advancing young swimmers to maturity through healthy stages of human growth and development.

As a USA-S Club coach, it is the challenge of the championship(s) that has dictated my approach to this question of quantity and/ or quality, speed and/or endurance? The difference in Club Championships and all other levels is the number and variety of events that these competitive swimmers need to race, the number of championship meets, and the number of days of meets during a championship season.

In my personal experience, the only sport that compares to championship swimming is championship wrestling, where athletes must wrestle multiple matches over days of competition to narrow the competitive field to the champions. And I must say that the competition is much more intense and demanding presently than during my athletic years.

The Club swimmer will race in preliminaries, (semi-finals), consolation finals and finals to win a championship at the national/ international levels. In state competitions, swimmers will race through long sessions of individual preliminaries and finals over (at least) three days, plus relay competition. Competition can be over 5 days at national meets and 8 days in the Olympic format.

Now – assuming that a team has a presence at championships, there will be a high endurance requirement, both physically and mentally, to be in winning form on the final day/session of competition. Thus, endurance needs consume a significant portion of the training season, or year(s), depending on the desired and expected level of competition.

Some research suggests that the best age ranges for development of aerobic capacity are between 12 and 15 years of age; therefore, this is another factor of responsibility for some club coaches.

This can be accomplished with a variety of approaches, but this work is important in the greater scheme of things for club swimmers. To negate this factor is to reduce the "odds" that a swimmer can be as accomplished through multiple championship meets over days and weeks of competition.

That said, studies show that the aerobic/VO2 Max systems will reach a threshold level which can be maintained through high speed/intensity training without sacrifice to endurance, providing that full attention has been given to the endurance phase during the training season/year(s). Understand, endurance training has a training effect of elevated mental consciousness as well as the physical adaptations.

Most competitive swimming programs select a specific meet for championship performance and try to "taper" for THE specific meet.

This works well if the swimmer has only one championship meet for which they are focused. But for most Club teams, there are multiple championship meets throughout a season which swimmers must:

1. Compete respective to Team score(s)

2. Compete at several levels for athletes that participate in multiple levels (club, high school, etc)

3. Qualify for, and compete at faster championship meets

4. Perform at the last of a championship series of meets, which will be more days of competition—5 to 8 days—and still be team scored

As stated above, providing the training program has given sufficient time and training tasks for VO2 Max endurance and muscular endurance, this endurance quality will be maintained through weeks, and even as much as a couple of months, of high intensity race specific training and racing. The formula that I have used to accomplish faster performance(s) as my teams move through championship series of meets is as follows:

- Set a date to transition from VO2 Max endurance training to race specific training. We like to allow about 3 days of recovery and technical emphasis swimming to make a good transition from VO2 Max to race specific training. We call this portion of the season *Peak Performance*. Other good nomenclatures might be Race Specific or Championship Training. At this time of the season(s), we give more rest and recovery between repetitions that are at (or approach) 100% effort. We do "broken swims" and straight swims racing and for time to simulate the challenges of actual races. We use resistance followed by "up and out" repetitions/races/ swims for time to *overcome neurological inhibition*. These are examples, but we do anything we can think of to create more speed or racing ability.

- Meets are part of the solution; not part of the problem during the Peak Performance stage of training and competition(s). We like that swimmers are racing at our Club meets, High School meets, YMCA meets, and more during peak performance. We understand that swimmers are at 100% effort when they are racing—and however much they race is good for this time in the season. This approach eliminates the Club coaches' attitude that other meets are a detriment to the Club coaches' ability to prepare athletes for Club championships.

- Typically, following the weekends we emphasize recovery and technique for a day. We then elevate the training back to high intensity levels (fast repetitions with recovery) and dry land exercise, <u>for half the number of days</u> between the last meet and the next meet. We also go back on the normal practice schedule regarding weekly attendance. After half of the days, we begin to gradually reduce the volume and intensity again until the upcoming competitive meet. We also return to "one a day" weekly attendance at the halfway point.

We want to accomplish numerous objectives during Peak Performance.

1. Practice with speed and technique that is specific to racing goals.

2. Make practice more challenging (physically and mentally) than they will experience at their meets.

3. *Overcome Neurological Inhibition.*

4. Be at the stroke length and stroke rate that are necessary to achieve the efficiency and speed that will be required to race, such that swimmers can accomplish their goals.

5. Build mental confidence through specific practice and mental training/visualization/breath.

6. Isolate practice on racing details such as starts, turns, and finishes at race speeds.

Now – there is not a specific period of time to stay in the respective training segments:

- Technical and aerobic build-up,

- VO2 Max endurance,

- Peak Performance.

It really depends on several factors:

1. National/international qualifiers and potential finalist(s)

2. State level competitors

3. Local level competitors

4. New swimmers to year around swimming

The coach may have athletes on a 4-year plan if there are potential Olympic Trials qualifiers.

The coach might break it down to the weeks/months of short and long course seasons if the athletes are expected to be competitive within a state level.

The coach might choose to break down a year into three training periods; that is, September through early December, late December through March, and April through mid-August.

What matters is that there are three phases to the training cycles and that adequate experience is scheduled to allow for the following:

1. Technical and Aerobic Build-up – During the first phase, we want to imprint appropriate techniques into the nervous system and build aerobic capacity to have readiness for VO2 Max training. Our goal is to target most of the swimming at heart rates 140 to 160 beats per minute. We normally count beats for 6 seconds and multiply times 10.

2. VO2 Max – Develops high intensity endurance such that the athlete can race in multiple events, over multiple sessions, over multiple days. Heart Rate objectives are 160 to 190 beats per minute.

3. Peak Performance – Race specific intensity with recovery encourages and allows for repetitions at maximum speed. Heart rate objectives are greater than or equal to 190 beats per minute. Active recovery heart rate objectives are equal to or less than 130 beats per minute in training sets. Passive recovery heart rate objectives are equal to, or less than 90 beats per minute to expect the greatest speed on repetitions following recovery.

There are methods and schemes for training which are different and effective. Planning training according to energy systems is popular. Presentations have shown color-coded planning such that certain time and attention is given to the various energy system categories for specific amounts of time over hours/days/weeks/ months and even years.

There are computer programs which will provide schedules and planning for performance that (essentially) will "insure" the athlete will perform according to a predictable result if the athlete works specific to the plan(s).

This is understood and there is no argument to that thinking.

HOWEVER, for the typical USA-S club swimmer who competes year around for as long as 10 years possibly, a multitude of variables exist (and happen) where planning specificity can bring more confusion for athletes, coaches, and families. Some changes are:

- Growth stages

- Changes in physiology specific to female and male development

- Social changes, especially during teen years.

- Psychological changes as swimmers move from the fun of racing, to the seriousness of goal setting, to pressures from others (families, coaches, peers), to the joy of the sport again.

- Perspective as it relates to life in general.

- Performance plateaus, which are somewhat normal, with many changing variables.

- Possible coaching changes with progression and development.

These changes may not exist for the coach and swimmer who are focused on seasonal training for a limited number of years. THIS IS THE POINT in covering USA-S Club swimming in more depth than training as it pertains to other organizations. I acknowledge that more specificity is reasonable for seasonal training and for specific ages of athletes. But it is different for USA-S Club coaches and athletes.

The same swimmer is most likely to compete in freestyle events from 100 yards/meters to the mile within one meet. The Club swimmer is likely to compete in all strokes and/or individual medley.

We have used the 400 Individual Medley and the 500 Freestyle as the theme to training in our program(s). This does not mean that all of our swimmers are necessarily competitive at those events. It does mean that all of our swimmers have training and racing exposure to those events.

Swimmers who tend toward the longer endurance events can swim those and swimmers who tend toward shorter events can swim those from that training. And – swimmers have a good background on which college coaches can train them for high levels of specificity.

For training, endurance is the higher physiological priority for us versus speed. We do consider speed as (somewhat) innate; thus, the coach can make a larger difference training endurance than speed.

That said, we do acknowledge speed, and work hard to increase strength and power, to maximize length in strokes, to have the hips in the right place at the right time for "timing," and to *overcome neurological inhibition* during peak performance planning.

We believe in splitting races and descending splits in distance races for efficiency and to allow our swimmers the best chance to win races in the end. And so, we practice accordingly.

For most races we divide the race into quarters. We encourage swimmers to swim the 1st quarter with natural flow and without unnecessary force. We want them to be very competitive in the 2nd quarter of the race such that they are in positions to win by the end of the 2nd quarter – or the halfway point. We want them to build speed in the 3rd quarter in order to hold the time on the 3rd split. We want them to be able and "inspired" to give their full 100% effort during the 4th quarter of the race to try to win the race.

We want the 2nd split of a race to be within 2 seconds of the first split, the 3rd split to be equal, and the 4th split to be the second fastest split of the race.

We call the 1st quarter "the technique of the race," the 2nd quarter "the speed of the race," the 3rd quarter "the guts of the race," and the 4th quarter "the thrill of the race."

For races of 500, 1000, or 1650 yards we want swimmers to get into the race pace (with respect to stroke length and stroke rate) in the 2nd 100, and to descend at certain stages of the race. We want the 2nd split to be within 3 seconds of the first split.

Splitting uses early speed naturally, uses energy cost efficiently and allows the best chance for using the best energy at the end of the race – a time in the race when racing vulnerabilities often exist. This strategy always keeps in mind that one must have a chance to win by the halfway point in the race to have a realistic belief that they will win. This does not mean that the swimmer needs to be winning at the halfway point. *The swimmer needs to be close enough in the race to believe they can win in the end.*

We like to determine and discuss "build points" in races at specific lap counts and use the lap counters as signals to build. For example: For the mile (short course), build points will be at the 19th, 39th, and 59th turns to finish. Race awareness might change this slightly but those are general build points. This prevents the need to shake lap counters over and over or to chase swimmers the length of the pool to "speed them up."

This also takes advantage of the reality that emphasis in the preparation has been relative to endurance.

Altogether, this chapter has been to make a case for the USA-S club coach to be in a somewhat different preparation paradigm than coaches in YMCA, High School, and Collegiate or Professional categories. Therefore, presentations about training should note specificity to the overall circumstances and differentiate rather than take the position that training for a given athlete will be appropriate for all athletes.

It should also be noted here that training is also according to facility circumstances, allowed training time, balance according to extremes in training and recovery, the availability and planning as it pertains to dry land training, group training experience, and other situational factors. In a 50-year career, I have trained USA-S Club swimmers in all of the following situations:

- Adequate pool time, inadequate pool time, no (evening) pool time

- Adequate dry land facilities, inadequate dry land facilities, no dry land facilities

- Decent pools and poor pools (I have never had an excellent pool)

- Training outdoors (regardless of outside temperatures)

- Training indoors and dealing with chloramines, poor ventilation, hot water, etc.—and when those elements were not factors

USA-S club coaches make the most of their circumstances they have and they plan for success using what they have. You are to be complimented for the hours you work, the patience you show, the adaptability of your lives and your dedication to your athletes.

4 — The Mental Game
("No Brain, No Gain")

Jack Nelson, a very accomplished coach and a wonderful motivator of the great Ft. Lauderdale Swim Team, had the following statement written on their team T-shirts for many years:

The Body Can Achieve
What the Mind Believes

During my early years of coaching, I required swimmers to maintain notebooks. The notebooks had sections for goals and objectives, a log of practices and comments, meet performance(s), and attendance. I would collect the logs weekly and return them with my comments on Mondays. This practice was GREAT for the mental game, and it was a very good way for me to communicate individually with swimmers. Numerous swimmers have later stated that they used their own notebooks to guide them as coaches after they finished competitive swimming for themselves.

But—it was an extremely time consuming endeavor for me. As teams became larger and my time became less, I used other ways to achieve similar coaching goals. Today, technology offers ways to achieve success at the mental game which may be preferable.

Jack Nelson's T-shirt statement embodies the mental game at its essence. It seems simple enough, and it is; however, the quest to achieve a state of mind for which there is an inner knowledge that provides confidence in athletes, that they will accomplish the desired results, can be one of many obstacles throughout the development of themselves – over years of time. Some factors are:

1. Nervousness > anxiety > fear

2. Respective levels of competition and ages

3. Changes in body type, physiology, technique, training, etc.

4. Goal setting – and belief, or lack of it

5. Preparation, or not – Connecting it

6. The Support Group – Family, teammates, coaches, others

7. Life its own-self – adaptations to stages of life

8. Process vs. random "Effort"

9. Artist vs. Engineer intelligence – and personality

10. Attention span

It has always been interesting to me that young children (most often) are attracted to competitive swimming because they want to race with other people who like to swim to reach an end. It might be across the pool, or the length of the pool, or more. The simple act of trying to get to the chosen end before other children is fun. It seems to me, if we keep the fun of the activity as simple as that, there might not be a "mental game."

But—at some point, certain result elements are attached to the races with respect to performance. The first is that parents and coaches attach their respective behaviors to the "winners." Then there is time associated with the race. Then there are challenges of "racing up" to equal levels of competition. Then money is invested to gain advantages with coaching, facilities, time, etc. Then travel and college are added to the mix. So the quest goes on and there are more and more challenges, most of which tend to change the element of fun in the race and to create the requirements for a "mental game."

That is not to imply that the aforementioned elements are negatives. All the while, this young racer is developing and maturing to become a strong adult in so many ways. They become complete competitive athletes after all. They become effective adults in a competitive world.

Once it is decided that a young racer will become part of a swim team, and race according to a structured format of competition, the journey begins. The first element of the mental game shows itself.

"It is good to have an end to journey towards, but it is the journey that matters in the end." Ursula K LeGuin

1. Nervousness, about whether the swimmer will be able to win and soon, whether the swimmer will "better their time." For some it becomes the perception that "winning is bettering one's time." Regardless, emotional responses result from nervousness, which can evolve to greater physical feelings which might be considered being anxious. Anxiety is defined as "a nervous 'disorder' characterized by excessive uneasiness and apprehension, typically with compulsive behavior." This problem can cause confusion in one's thinking that can displace the goal of racing to a successful result. Anxiety can evolve into fear—a feeling of anxiety concerning an outcome of something, or the safety or well-being of someone. In the movie *Point Break,* the character called Bodhi (Patrick Swayze) said this to his counter-character played by Keanu Reeves before Reeves was about to jump from an airplane: *"Fear causes apprehension and apprehension causes your greatest fear to come true."* Fear can be a cause for the fight or flight response at a moment of time, allowing for a fast race, but it cannot be used as a motivating factor for competing well over time. So how is this avoided?

    •   Preparation – Excellent preparation provides self-confidence.

    •   Perspective – the athlete, sometimes with the help of others, perceives the race as it is; that is, simply a race, with the help of others as part of your solution, to give 100% of your best effort at the given point in time and place. The athlete should understand, the task is simply "what it is," nothing more or less.; 200 meters is the same distance of swimming whether it is practice, an early-season meet, or championships. Assuming excellent preparation, there is no need to make more of it than it is (physically). It is only "the mind" that might make it seem different.

- Mental Focus – the athlete should be 100% "in the moment" respective to thoughts; that is, now performance is not dependent on others. It is not for family, or coaches, or teammates, or spectators, or anything else. Performance is an opportunity for the athlete. Others might be motivation or good reminders, etc., leading up to the race, but at the moment(s) in time of the race itself, it is only the athlete with respect to himself/herself. All energy of mind, body, and spirit can be given by the athlete to himself/herself. Let it be.

2. Generally, there is (almost) none of number 1 when swimmers are competing with other swimmers they know to be slower than themselves. When competing with equals, there might be some nervousness, but confidence is normally okay in this situation. It is usually when the competition is unknown, or when there is a knowledge from the beginning that the competition is faster, that swimmers experience something between anxiety and fear. The mental game in this instance is to give positive energy to the situation. It is the "glass half full or half empty" that we so often hear described in terms of how one thinks. The athlete has a choice in this. He can choose to give himself positive energy by keeping focus on what he wants to happen, or he can choose to give himself negative energy by keeping his focus on what he does not want to happen. It is that simple. I did not say it is that easy. But – one can choose the thoughts that will be dominant in performance.

3. Changes – As swimmers advance through the process of maturity and age, they change. The first significant change

for most swimmers happens when they reach the stage of puberty. There is sometimes growth and sometimes not, there are hormonal changes in the athletes' physiology, there are significant socialization changes – different for boys and girls, and there are psychological changes. I could go on, but suffice to say that the accumulation of change can have dynamic effects on the mental game. It is normal for adaptation to change(s) to take time. And, it is improbable for athletes to be altogether mature through the process of change, which is "the norm" for teenage athletes. COACHES, parents, and other adults need to be helpful during this stage of development for athletes. Judgment is NOT helpful.

Teaching swimmers about what is happening at this time is helpful. Offering and building the knowledge of how to behave and be patient, always offering the knowledge that: a) doing the right thing(s) will ultimately give the best results, and b) stay competitive because the sport is competitive swimming. Help them believe that they will become stronger, more enduring, wiser, and be able to help others if they remain 'on course.'

4. Goal Setting: Goals are good and Goals are bad. Goals are good when they provide a "road map" for the journey of preparation to achieve the goal(s). Goals are good when they give discipline to the process of preparation. Goals are good when they are detailed and complete such that they give you feedback while you prepare. Goals are good when they are realized. Goals are bad if they are incomplete; that is, if they do not have relevant split times, if they do not state intent for technical perfection, if goal elements are not practiced deliberately, and if they cause one to think only about the goal in the moment of performance rather than process—and thusly cause negative pressure. Goals are bad when they are not realized if a negative attitude results from having had the goal and failing to reach it. ALL of this must be taught to

athletes by COACHES when doing goal setting. Athletes need to understand the positive and negative aspects of goals – and how to use them properly.

5. Preparation – is at the core of the mental game. Preparation is the heart of the mental game. Preparation is the cardio-pulmonary system of the mental game. Preparation is the skeleton of the mental game. Preparation is the STRENGTH of the mental game. Without full and complete preparation in every way over time, there is not a mental game. The mental game of the athlete comes from all things; that is, deliberate practice of racing factors, training the physiology of the athlete, learning perspective, mental visualization, nutrition, rest, relationships – and any other item which affects performance. To the extent that an athlete fails in an aspect of performance, the athlete is vulnerable to some degree of failure accordingly. This I say over time. It is possible to have good performance – in a moment – with poor preparation; however, it is not possible to realize one's potential over years of time without dedication to full and complete preparation. Finally, the athlete must <u>connect</u> the intelligence of fact(s) that the preparation is for a specific reason. For example: the swimmer must realize that an accomplishment in practice is not of significance unless it is applied to the race for which he/she is practicing. This might be turning techniques, or repetition times, or underwater dolphin kicking – but – if the swimmer is not practicing to do what is expected in the race, it is not likely to happen in the stressful segment of the race. Likewise, if the swimmer has practiced according to the race expectations, he/she is most likely to do so in the race. It must be connected intellectually.

6. The Support Group – Family, Teammates, and Coaches, Outside Friends – The mental game becomes a mirage of inputs into the brain. As athletes begin the early stage of development, all of the "support group" elements bombard the individual swimmer's consciousness. They all mean well.

But, most often, it is more information than the swimmer can compartmentalize at that stage. The typical example is:

- A swimmer has their individual objectives for a particular race at the swim meet in mind from the practice they have been doing. On the way to a meet, or even at the meet, one of the parents adds a "parental suggestion" for the race. During warm up the coach, or coaches offer general racing insights, then a friendly teammate tells the swimmer something else "to help," and finally the swimmer visits a coach at the last minutes before the race for any thoughts on the race.

Now this swimmer has more information leading up to the race than they can possibly use to focus clearly on the upcoming race. With too much information and a desire to compete well, the result is usually nervousness, or anxiety, or fear. Of course, everybody means well, but they have actually become part of the problem rather than part of the solution. Another example is:

- That same swimmer hears the following before they race: From the parent – "I love to watch you swim." From the teammate(s) – "You've been great in practice. I know you can be awesome in this race." From the coach in warm up, "Y'all have really been great at practice going into this meet. Let's focus on being your best and race tough." And finally, in the last instruction before the race, the coach reminds the athlete to build speed during the race and finish in a ray of splendor.

This scenario allows the swimmer to keep their own focus for the race, while imagining that they will increase racing speed toward a finishing effort that might win the race. The mental game has been served. The swimmer's support group can be very motivating and helpful to the swimmer, but they can also be 'somewhat' of a hindrance. Eventually, the swimmer will learn to focus clearly, regardless of distractions. Swimmers will gain perspective such that they understand that all of their support group wants them to perform well. Swimmers will learn to intellectually compartmentalize information which allows them to be their best. When swimmers have 'super' prepared in all phases of practice, it allows them to be motivated, trust their instincts, be free of anxiety and race to win and/or achieve their goals. This is the ideal in the mental game, and how the support group can be tremendously helpful.

7. Life its own-self – USA Club swimmers experience many significant changes over (possibly) 10 years of training and competition. Illnesses and injuries happen. Through the years they grow (or others grow and they grow later), their physiologies change (male- and female-related), they progress through many levels of competition (especially in championships), they change socially (as they try to find compatible peer groups), they change intellectually as education changes them with age, they morph through changes with parents and other relationships, and more. Periods of plateau are fairly usual as swimmers live their lives. They have to learn to adapt to these life changes. For some, the ability to keep a healthy perspective, to allow time for adaptations for themselves, and to continue to believe in themselves (and others) is necessary to progress in the sport. Coaches and parents need to help swimmers through these changes and stages of development. Youthfulness is (most often) counterintuitive to behaviors necessary to adapt. For the adults in their lives, patience is required to help them. Adaptation can take years for some. For others, it happens in months. Regardless, it is never easy for the athlete, nor those who love them. Emotions often contribute to difficulties. The results are that forgiveness and healing are necessary in life. In the end, it is mostly good for all concerned if the athlete continues in the sport. Challenges and adaptations are helpful. When all is done, almost all will reflect such that they consider their lives in sport as being tremendously joyful and valuable.

8. Process vs. Random Effort – In the beginning (ages 7 – 9),

effort is mostly random; that is, swimmers have been exposed to a minimum of learning and training. Following that, some young swimmers start to use learning and training, some don't. Some are natural at racing while others are natural at learning swimming and racing. But, for all other than about 2% of swimmers, swimming is counterintuitive. At the foundation of swimming skills is rhythmic breathing as it pertains to water. Swimmers instinct is to hold their breath when faces are submerged; then try to breathe out and in when the face is above the waters' surface. Swimmers are challenged with exchanging oxygen and carbon dioxide equally with given head movement. It is instinctive to pull and push water to propel forward; however, it is equally (or more) important to combine hip movement with the reaching arm to move forward with power and efficiency. For breaststroke and butterfly it is most important to have the hips in the right place at the right time. Then there is training. It is VERY important to practice at race speeds and to use strategies that one intends to use while racing to expect it to happen in a swim meet. Altogether, it is not random practice that helps swimmers to succeed in races. It is deliberate practice, specific to intent. It is a process. The process needs to be "imprinted" into the nervous system, the athletes' physiology, and into the intelligence of the swimmer. This process is ideal when it is an agreement between the coach and the athlete.

9. Artists and Engineers – and Personality: Broadly, there were two predominant types of individuals for whom I realized, early in my coaching career, that I needed to coach differently. And, there were two swimmers who taught me about these types. The first is what I will call the "artist." Her name was Kim Vogel. Kim was a wonderful competitor. I noticed that in my communications with her, I was most successful when I spoke to her in terms of feel for the water, the flow of her body's movement in the water, the feel of accelerations and decelerations, etc. Kim was what I would describe as an

emotional swimmer. She was an excellent competitor when she was happy and focused. I learned that it was helpful to her when I could get her to imagine an artistic experience having to do with water when she seemed to be lacking in performance.

The engineer type was Danny Morris, who swam about the same time frame as Kim (the early 1980s). Danny was very analytical about swimming. He eventually became a US Naval Academy graduate. Danny liked to know about the angles of his arms and hands in movement, reasons for propulsive force, body lines for efficiency, physiology, etc. He wanted to have race strategy so he could choose the best times during a race to stay efficient—but win. Danny was spirited, but not what I would call emotional about training or racing. He wanted to practice according to his racing goals. Both were wonderful to coach, but as their coach, I needed to learn their respective attributes. My experience with them has been helpful to a multitude of swimmers that came after them.

10. Attention Span – One of the great elements of club coaching is that the coach works with swimmers, in most cases, for as much as a decade. Swimmers come to year-round competitive swimming (generally) about 8 years old and leave for college when they are about 18. Attention spans often change as swimmers change from one level of maturity to another. It is normal to experience swimmers who have wonderful attention when they are pre-puberty and become completely distracted by the challenges of teen years. But the coach can use tools to affect attention.

Captain James Flanagan, my English literature teacher in high school, was a master at language, and knew how to use his voice to gain attention. He used every element of tone and volume to command attention. He used language accents. Occasionally, I would lose focus on the actual content of the subject in class, as I enjoyed his presentation skills. This is a trait of teaching I have tried to emulate over time to keep attention to practice and meet performance. To do the unexpected is also valuable in keeping attention. Unexpected facial expressions, use of hands and arms, your movement among the athletes are good tools. A coach can even fake happiness or anger to gain attention. That is not abuse – but a controlled emotional response to lack of attention. It is also important to give confidence to athletes that you know the subject you are presenting. When a practice group or an individual has that confidence, they are more likely to be attentive to your presentation of it.

Altogether, swimmers have a basic desire to be attentive most of the time. Attention is the one aspect of coaching that can be taken personally, while the lack of attention may have nothing to do with the coach. It is more likely that the athlete simply has something else to dominate their attention. For the USAS club coach, you are better to realize that you have that decade to get your point across to the athlete.

"The Body Can Achieve
What the Mind Believes."

The coaches' job is to work toward this end for as long as they coach athletes. It will come and go for them, but the coach needs to keep it as a constant goal – always.

Note: Another thing that Coach Jack Nelson taught me when I was very young was this ,in his words: "I am a professional in my field; therefore, I get up, regardless of how early, and shower, shave, put on the clothes for my profession, and go to work, full of positive energy. No swimmer will be able to use my behavior as an excuse to be tired. I am professional like any other banker or doctor or lawyer or anything else." From the time that I heard Jack say those words, I woke up early to shower and shave and present myself with energy to the swimmers. I coached this way for the remainder of my career, and I think it was a good habit professionally.

5 — No Limits

Balance: "Search the outer limits for greatness, but return to the norm for rest – before the next great event." – Dudley Duncan

There are no limits, in my opinion.

The longest training amounts that I have heard to be given are of Vladimir Salnikov, the first swimmer under 15 minutes in 1500 meters (14:58.27). Rumors were of him swimming up to 30,000 meters in days of training. He was competitive into his 30's.

In the USA, I heard of Dick Shoulberg giving 16,000 meter Individual Medley practice swims.

I have also heard of National level competitors training under 30,000 meters per week for shorter events.

In the year prior to Mary T. Meagher's 1981 world record swims in the 100/200 meter butterfly, she was known to do 3000 meter butterfly swims faster than most women could swim the distance freestyle. This was a statement from her coach (Dennis Pursley) that year—as I remember hearing it.

She was coached by Bill Peak in the year of her phenomenal world record swims. Bill's concentration was on IM training, but I believe the year prior was very impactful on the world record performances.

The year prior to Cynthia (Sippy) Woodhead swimming the 200 meter freestyle in world record time, she was training for distance events at 20,000 meters in a day at times during the season. I would offer that the year prior was impactful to the following year of the world record performance.

The boundaries are (obviously) widely debated as to pros and cons for various types of training. For my own programs, the most training meters that I have given has been toward 100,000 yards/meters per week for some time (December 1987 until Memorial Day Weekend – 1988). The least that I have given has been in the area of 36,000 yards/meters per week for some time. In this, I am referring to the time of a season when VO2 Max was the physiological objective.

Whatever "the coach" decides, the following elements should be considered:

- Gradualness: that is, the most challenging portion of the season should be reached through gradual progressions which allow the swimmers' physiology to adapt along the way. Adaptation typically reaches a beginning stage at about 3 weeks, and the coach can be fairly certain that full adaptation will occur in 6 weeks. When the training group reached 100,000 per week, we used the entire fall months to reach that level.

- Balance: If the coach is going to challenge athletes with extremes, they must also share the intent to balance it out. We used 12 practice sessions per week to reach 100,000. The following year we trained 6 sessions per week and maintained about 40,000 per week. Both seasons were successful (especially mid to longer distance events in 1988 and shorter to mid distance events in 1989), but it was important for me to communicate to the athletes that they would experience less after they had achieved more.

- Discipline: To train high numbers of sessions and/or high amounts of mileage requires a disciplined commitment for swimmers in the training group, the coach, and families of the respective athletes.

- Communication: The coach must communicate the following to all concerned –

  - A rationale for the training amounts,

  - A specific time period for which the training regimen will last,

- The goal(s) and objective(s) of the training,

- How balance will be achieved after the training phase is complete,

- The need for families to be part of the athletes' solutions respective to rest, nutrition, and general support.

- <u>Technical</u>: When training greater than "normal" amounts, the coach must have strategies to maintain technical awareness and prevent performance degradation. This can be done with specificity in warm up swims, swim downs, set objectives that include specific speeds at specific stroke counts, and giving feedback to swimmers during practices.

Note: VACS took 15 swimmers to USA Junior Nationals in 1988 and placed 3rd at the women's USAS Short Course National Championships in 1989.

———

USRPT (Ultra Short Race Pace Training) has been popularized by Michael Andrew and his father/coach Peter Andrew. Literature on the methods has been, and is being, developed pertaining to the underlying philosophy for training, the methods, and related results. From a "club coaching perspective," my personal opinion is that this methodology is overly limiting for average USA club (developing) swimmers; that is, according to these following elements:

1. Club swimmers are dependent on the concept of deliberate practice such that the swimmers' nervous systems are imprinted with myelin sheath(s) to include the spinal cord and brain through appropriate repetition,

2. VO2 Max capacity needed for USA club meet sessions, especially with preliminary and finals formats day after day, which often require swimmers to compete in back to back events of varying strokes and distances,

3. Physiological and coordination characteristics which are developed through a programmed approach to exercise on dry land.

4. As a practical matter, club coaches are typically challenged with numbers and capabilities in lanes that do not lend themselves to year around USRPT training methods.

In our programs at QUEST Swimming, we have used the term *Peak Performance* to designate portions of time, or the training season, to designate race specific training. Race Specific Training has a lower yardage/mileage expectation, but the adaptation expectation is specific to the race challenges of a typical meet situation or circumstance.

To use a term that I defined in an earlier chapter, the specific goal of this training is to "*overcome neurological inhibition;*" that is, to practice at speeds, or with resistance, which will cause the swimmer to be faster than the race expectation. Remember, all of us have, internalized in our nervous systems, what we consider to be normal expectations for physical accomplishments. This fact places limits on our ability to accomplish certain feats. This is much like a "governor" to regulate speed on a school bus.

We sometimes observe people who overcome their limits in emergency situations. Most of us have heard stories of the older lady who lifts a car to rescue a person underneath.

I actually experienced this occurrence when my father was pinned under our car because it slipped from "the jack" (1953). My mother (and me at 5 years old) raised the car enough for my father to slip out. My mother would not have normally been able to raise the car that amount, but for that moment she *overcame neurological inhibition* to do so. I am sure that I was of zero help, but I was trying as hard as I could. Giving credit, my older sister also helped to pull on my Dad's legs to help remove him from under the car.

Race specific is also to practice the race scenario such that the actual race in the meet is automatic; that is, it happens without thought. Japanese samurai swordsmen refer to this mental state as *"Mushin."* The samurai idea here is, if you have to think to react, you will be dead at the hands (sword) of your opponent. To reach a stage of "non-thought" is the ideal – and – it is the objective in race specific training. The common phrase is that one needs to practice 10,000 times (correctly and in succession) to reach this stage of mental readiness. We are not sure exactly how many perfect repetitions one must accomplish to reach this state, but it is a lot.

Physiologically, it is described that a "myelin sheath" surrounds neural pathways which strengthen the habitual workings of muscle fiber when practice is achieved in regular succession. This will occur whether the athlete is performing well or poorly; therefore, it is ever important to perform <u>consistently</u> well.

So let's get back to the question: *<u>What are the limits of training</u>*? Specific to the club swimming coach, it is my belief that the coach should have an open mind regarding this question.

There was a season in my career when my highest level swimmers did not have evening pool time and they had 90 minutes in the morning before school on 3 mornings per week. We did a 4 hour practice on Saturday mornings which consisted of @ 60 minutes dry land, @ 60 minutes of water polo, @ 120 minutes of water interval training. We supplemented with an extensive weekly dry land program.

Our morning swims were focused on technique, speed, and resistance in the water since swimming endurance was unlikely from the amount of swimming we could achieve per week. This particular season was for the fall months from September to December; therefore, the swimmers had a good background of swimming mileage from the previous summer months. Those swimmers were quite successful at their December championship meet.

Evening dryland practices were:

Odd days

- Wheels[1] around the field house

- Wheels for time up the field house ramp to the second floor – for time – and run down stairs to return to the starting point

- Calisthenics routine on the pool deck and in the bleachers section

Even Days

- Running on a track—an aerobic run plus intervals

- Resistance training on a universal gym with stations (in a large storage closet under the bleachers)

- Dumbbells

- Jump Rope

The point of this example is that swimming athletes can be successful regardless of whether the coach is offering swimming at the lower end of the boundaries, or the upper end of the boundaries – and everything between. There simply needs to be good planning for adaptations and effective communication respective to the plan. We also limited competitive events in meets to 200 yards and less during those months when we only had morning time.

Now, the club coach also has the responsibility to prepare athletes for swimming at the collegiate levels. Since there are many collegiate coaches, and they vary greatly as to philosophies for training, there

---

1 Wheels are 2x4 pieces cut about 2 feet wide. I drilled a hole through them to accept an axle and attached lawn mower wheels on each end. The 2x4 pieces had carpet pieces attached to them. Swimmers would place their shins on them and pull themselves over a distance or up an incline for time. They used weight lifting gloves on their hands. I got the idea from the Reese brothers who were using them to train on stadium inclines for their college swimmers.

is wisdom for the club coach to test some boundaries of training for athletes; that is, to change seasonal plans for adaptations such that the athlete has a broad experience. This will prepare athletes for whatever training challenges they will experience in college or otherwise.

For most of my coaching experience, most of my plans have worked overall. There have been individual instances of "failure," but those were most often due to the fact that I was still learning the athlete, the athlete was experiencing physiological changes, or the athlete chose not to practice diligently within the plan.

———

The question of "what is the perfect amount" of training began to be debated and discussed much more when USA Swimming moved headquarters to Colorado Springs, Colorado, and more information on energy systems and recovery began to be published from the sport science department.

I was a physical education major in college and much of what was being published from USAS was familiar to me. It was all right and good. However, it was mostly specific to certain events, their length of time and distance -and respective preparation.

It did not take into account the physiological challenges of the typical club swimmer in the typical club meet(s) – in which swimmers compete for (at least) three days in events ranging in distances from 50 yards/meters to the mile (freestyle), all strokes, and in preliminary/finals sessions. This schedule is grueling. Truly! Also, at Olympic levels swimmers compete in preliminaries, semi-finals and finals, sessions if they are fast enough to qualify for all.

All of that said, the USAS club coach actually prepares swimmers for these total of swim meet events, including relays. Swimmers might compete as many as 18 times over three days or more. Often it is the case that a swimmers' best events are on the last day of competition. One needs to be able to compete as well on that last day as the first day.

The primary requirement for these meets is ENDURANCE. This specific endurance requirement is to be able to compete at the highest potential speed for the length of the distance of the event(s) on the last day of competition—after they have (already) done so for at least two days. Therefore, simple philosophies on exercise and recovery do not necessarily prepare the swimmers for this particular challenge.

Another piece to this puzzle is what is referred to as "the mental game." The mental game is more than being able to dig deep and tap into the will to win. It starts with preparation. The swimmer needs to experience similar circumstances in training and in meets leading up to championships. The swimmer needs to understand and have practiced efficiency in racing; that is, splitting the sections of races such that energy is used efficiently throughout the days and sessions of competition. The swimmer must keep perspective and control over emotions as the competition progresses through sessions and days. Finally, the swimmer needs to rise to the occasion of the all-important event at the end of the meet. In addition to individual performance, the swimmer's team might be in a team scored meet; this is an addition to the individual challenges the swimmers are enduring.

Another challenge for the club coach is that training groups can be large. In fact, it is typical to have 4 to 6 swimmers per lane of varying skills and capabilities. Early in my career, I coached a group of 64 swimmers in an 8 lane, 25 yard pool, between the ages of 10 and 18. Such numbers of swimmers in lanes and groups lends more to interval training than to race specificity. The coach is challenged with the best use of time and space to develop positive changes to individual physiologies and kinesthetic tendencies. Ultimately, coaches should dedicate (at least) a portion of seasons or years to race specificity, such that swimmers are given opportunities to compete (purely) and to *overcome neurological inhibition*. The coach should challenge swimmers during race specific training to move at equal or higher speeds than will be reached in races.

Generally, my seasonal plans have included a period of aerobic swimming involving over-distance or short interval swims where heart rates are between 140 – 160 beats per minute. This has been followed with a period of time dedicated to VO2Max development with higher speeds on short to medium intervals where heart rates would target between 170 – 190 beats per minute. Above 190 beats per minute will take the swimmer into anaerobic zones and cause the swimmer to fail in the set performance on VO2Max sets. That said, we would seek heart rates greater than 190 beats per minute during race specific training.

Examples of Practice Sets:

Aerobic (yards) – senior level
100 Butterfly – 1:30 – 200 Backstroke – 2:30 – 300 Breaststroke – 4:00 – 400 Freestyle – 5:00 – 400 Freestyle – 5:00 – 300 Backstroke – 3:45 – 200 Breaststroke – 3:00 – 100 Butterfly – 1:30

Note: Intervals might be slower or faster, depending on the respective speed capabilities of swimmers.

LeapFrog (or Indian Swim) – 30 minutes Freestyle: Swimmers line up in a line of 4 or 5, every other lane. The line swims out close together; that is, on the feet of the swimmer in front of them. There is a "passing" lane open next to each lane. When the line has swum 50 yards, the swimmer at the back of the line moves into the passing lane, passes the line and moves back at the front of the line. Now the new swimmer at the back moves to the passing lane, passes the line and moves over to lead the line. This continues for the entire 30 minutes, or for whatever total time is set for the swim.

VO2Max (yards for normal senior level swimmers, meters for world class swimmers)

Freestyle

Interval = 2:00
4 x 150 – 1 x 200
3 x 150 – 1 x 200
2 x 150 – 1 x 200
1 x 150 – 1 x 200
Interval = 1:00
4 x 75 – 1 x 100
3 x 75 – 1 x 100
2 x 75 – 1 x 100
1 x 75 – 1 x 100
Interval =:30
4 x 25 – 1 x 50
3 x 25 – 1 x 50
2 x 25 – 1 x 50
1 x 25 – 1 x 50

Heart Rates on shorter recovery swims are typically between 140 and 150.

For 200s-100s-50s Heart Rates should be 180 to 200.

Yards
10 x 225 Individual Medley – 3:00

Odd – 75 Butterfly, 75 Backstroke, 75 Breaststroke
Even
2 – 75 Butterfly, 50 Backstroke, 50 Breaststroke, 50 Freestyle
4 – 50 Butterfly, 75 Backstroke, 50 Breaststroke. 50 Freestyle
6 – 50 Butterfly, 50 Backstroke, 75 Breaststroke, 50 freestyle
8 – 50 Butterfly, 50 Backstroke, 50 Breaststroke, 75 Freestyle
10 – Recovery swim – odd lengths freestyle, even lengths backstroke (focus on rhythmic breathing)

Race Specific
Broken Swims for time:—yards

1 x 200/Broken with 10 seconds at 75, 10 seconds at 125, 10 seconds at 175 – 5:00 (Goal – Faster than best shaved meet performance time) @ 5:00
1 x 200 Recovery swim – @ 3:00
1 x 200/Broken with 10 seconds rest at same distances – 5:00 (Goal – Faster than best shaved meet performance) @ 5:00
2 x 200 Recovery swim – @ 3:00
1x 200/Broken with 10 seconds rest at each 50 – @ 5:00 (same goal)
3 x 200 Recovery swim – @ 3:00
1 x 200/Broken with 10 seconds rest at each 25 – 8 full blast sprints

On broken swims, the rest can be pre-subtracted and the time on the clock will be their time so the swimmers can read it, saving the coach calling out the times so they can watch for technical elements.

800 Recovery Swim – 200 Freestyle (10 kick switch), 200 Backstroke (10 kick switch), 200 Breaststroke (3 count glide – focus on breath), 200 front quadrant freestyle – focus on breath)

Up and Outs:
Races in heats according to 50s, 100s & 200s: Use diving well or designated lane(s) for recovery swimming:

Strokes of Choice (for TIME)
1 x 200
2 x 100
4 x 50
Recovery Swim = 800 (odd 100s swim, even 100s kick (back, right side, left side, back)
4 x 50
2 x 100
1 x 200

So back to the question of limits: Limits are according to the respective imagination and creativity of the coach's thinking and planning.

Swimmers can experience value in greater volume of training and lesser volume of training and everything in between.

That said, there is such a thing as "overtraining and under-training." The coach must keep a keen eye for over-training symptoms, listen to swimmers when they express themselves, and plan for recovery opportunities when a commitment is made to do more. Under-training is easy to recognize because swimmers will be overly energetic and they will inevitably struggle to "get home" in racing situations. When the coach develops a rationale for more than the amount of training to which the swimmers are accustomed, they must communicate that rationale and continue to reinforce the reason(s) as the training continues to progress. And – swimmers must be able to "see the light at the end of the tunnel;" that is, they should know when balance will be offered.

For example: In the season that I trained swimmers toward 100,000 yards/meters per week, they knew the date that we would complete that training – and – they knew the following year would be one practice per day throughout the next short course season. They knew that volume would be 36 – 40,000 yards/meters per week during the short course season that followed.

In performance, we were in the top 5 teams at Junior Nationals (short and long course) that year, we were represented by 12 swimmers from our program at Olympic Trials, and one made the Olympic Team. In the following short course season, our women's team placed 3rd at the USA Short Course National Championships – working off of the previous year's background and the one practice per day following it.

This discussion about respective volumes of training largely concerns swimmers in the later years of high school and from which swimmers develop out of progressive novice and age group experiences toward senior levels of training and competition.

There is also a paradigm which has changed, mostly in this century of time. World class swimmers now come much more from professional and collegiate levels and ages. It is difficult for high school aged swimmers to compete in the finals of the USA Olympic Trials and international competition. Their bodies and minds are still developing, their time is more limited with high school schedules, and their facilities for training are less ideal than colleges and those where professionals are training.

The USA club coach is now preparing swimmers for the next level – mostly. Occasionally, females might gain that level from club programs. Less occasionally, a male might reach that level. Those would be circumstances when club coaches might consider a plan for training toward more extreme boundaries, such as creating a 2-, 3-, or 4-year plan for the specific athlete.

Otherwise, the thesis of this chapter is to keep an open mind concerning the right way to train. Actually, many training methods can work. Simply _plan_ thoroughly and _constantly communicate_—specific to objectives and feedback on achievement—from beginning to end of the process.

Deliberate Practice are the two most important words concerning practice.

The coach is a very important "controlling" factor in this regard. The coach needs to be watching, and giving feedback on: stroke counts, times, turns, finishes, technical fundamentals, and more.

Deliberate Practice is easier when doing less. The coach is integral when doing more.

6 — Equipment

In September 1977, I was hired to start a competitive swimming program at the Vero Beach YMCA in Vero Beach, Florida, and in association with the Indian River Swim Team, which was located in the neighboring town of Ft. Pierce, Florida, and Indian River Community College (*now Indian River State College*). A 1972 Olympic coach, and a great person, named Jim Montrella, was the Head Coach at Indian River. He hired me for the job.

One day during the fall, Jim came to Vero Beach to visit and observe a practice that I was leading. On this day, the group was using hand paddles during a set. The hand paddles had rubber straps placed on the paddles so the middle finger was placed to the front of the paddle and another was placed to the back of the paddle to secure the wrist of the arm to the paddle.

These hand paddles happened to have been invented by Jim Montrella. He owned a manufacturing and distribution company called Modern Concepts, Inc. When Jim saw the swimmers using the hand paddles while swimming, he suggested to me that I have the swimmers remove the wrist bands from the paddles.

He explained that his original invention was without the wrist bands and that the paddles were invented to improve stroke mechanics in freestyle and backstroke. The idea was that the paddle would give feedback to the swimmer if there were stroke flaws. Specifically, the paddle would change positions on the hands of the swimmer if a hand entry was wrong, if the hand exit from the water was early or wrong, if the hand traveled too much to the inside or outside under the body, if the hand failed to follow though properly in the stroke, or if there was inadequate hand acceleration through the line of pull to keep the paddle pressed to the hand(s). The paddle would actually be pulled from the hand oftentimes if the stroke flaw was severe enough.

Jim further explained to me that the hand paddles functioned as he had imagined; however, the feedback he received from swim coaches was that the paddles were no good because they did exactly what they were invented to do. That is, they changed positions on their hands and came off. Coaches made an adaptation to the paddles by drilling holes into the rear of the paddles so wristbands could be placed into them. Jim learned that the paddles were not selling without the wristbands, but they would sell with the wristbands, so coaches could use them for resistance training – and not the original intent for which the hand paddles were designed.

Learning this, I have never again used paddles with wrist straps.

Equipment can be used for more than one purpose, but it is preferable to me to use equipment to strengthen stroke mechanics while *overcoming neurological inhibition* when possible.

Another example is the use of pull buoys that are placed at the crotch, between the thighs. I believe that pull buoys placed at that body location *falsely* elevates the hips; that is, the need to use upper body balance pressure (points) to elevate the hips is negated. This is shown by swimmers who can pull with a buoy between the legs faster than they can swim.

I prefer the Finis Pull Buoy which is placed at the ankles. The buoy is designed as a figure 8. Its use necessitates that swimmers pay attention to upper body balance points and pressure(s) to maintain a horizontal bodyline while swimming. The Finis Buoy can also be used for kicking, and I prefer them to kickboards for kicking over distance, because they keep a better position in the water.

I do like kickboards for kicking fast over short distances because one can produce faster foot speed with them. When kicking over distance with kickboards, immature swimmers tend to keep improper body positions and to become lost in conversation (often) while kicking.

Once, I observed a graduate of QUEST Swimming (Jeff Newkirk), who was attending the University of Texas and was being coached by Eddie Reese, accomplish a very effective kick set on a kickboard while home from college. He was doing the set on his own; that is, without teammates to distract him. While Jeff made good use of the kickboard in that instance, I have rarely been satisfied with longer distance kick sets using kickboards. I mostly prefer kicking in various body positions without apparatus when kicking over distances beyond sets of under 75 yards. Examples are:

- Kicking streamlined on the back

- Kicking on a side. Right and left, nose up and nose down

- Kicking underwater

- Combinations

I like equipment for training. It adds variety to practice(s) and it serves to *overcome neurological inhibition*, to increase power, to challenge oxygen consumption, to understand the relationships between stroke length and stroke rate, to compete, and to know "desire."

BUT, use of equipment often means that swimming efficiency, or economy, is sacrificed for the physical work to produce physiological results. When this is the case, the coach should follow the use of equipment with an emphasis on attention to efficiency elements. This is simply a "reset" of mental focus and neurological mapping to keep efficiency as a foundation for everything else presented in training.

For many years, roughly 25 years of my career as a swim coach, senior level swimmers who normally trained 9 sessions per week, used equipment in morning sessions. The equipment used in those morning sessions was surgical tubing, weight baskets, water buckets on a pulley system, vertical kicking with scuba weight belts or with free weights, and fins for speed. I used these equipment items to motivate swimmers to attend mornings, to provide a graduation from "typical" equipment to something perceived to be "more" sophisticated training, to encourage teamwork, team spirit, and to *overcome neurological inhibition.*

This took significant extra time for me to set up and break down the equipment so it would be ready for swimmers to use when they arrived, make good use of it during their practice time, and break it down/clean up after swimmers left. I chose to do this, as opposed to swimmers doing it when they arrived and after they left, to make the best use of their training time—for them. During the latter years of my career when time was a greater challenge for me, I needed to find other ways to achieve many of the objectives of the "equipment" mornings. I think I was successful at doing this; however, the equipment mornings were highly motivating for most swimmers, and for me.

Equipment is good. It changes the dynamic of "swimming laps." But the coach also has a responsibility to know the potential downsides of equipment use, to observe carefully, and to communicate with swimmers to prevent potential stroke flaws or injuries that can happen with the use of equipment. As stated in an earlier chapter, swimming is a balance of stroke length and stroke rate. To the extent that practice planning chooses stroke rate as a priority over stroke length, there is the possibility that:

1. The swimmer will gain the sense that stroke rate is a higher priority over stroke length—when stroke length should (mostly) be established prior to stroke rate in performance.

2. The swimmer can fail to distinguish between physical discomfort necessary to accomplish the task and physical discomfort that is injurious.

The coach can usually tell the difference between effort that is efficient and effort that is simply effort for the sake of effort. The coach has the responsibility to look and to see those differences.

There is also the potential for a swimmer to compromise "feel for the water" when using equipment. For natural swimmers, the feel for the water seems to be innate. Natural swimmers are (probably) about 1% to2% of the swimming population; therefore, the coach has a responsibility to re-establish a feel for the water following equipment experiences.

Fist gloves or fist closed swimming is a good example of a way to re-establish the feel for the water. By taking away the hands as an element of movement and then giving them back, there is an accentuated feel for the water on the hands. Stroke count goals, and sets where stroke count combined with time goals are effective. Swimming "chicken wing" and then gradually lengthening arms and hands is effective for feeling the water. This is also good for timing the hips to the recovery of arms to create greater stroke length and feel for the water.

Use of equipment has everything to do with the creativity of coaches in using it. One use often gives an idea for another use. It may be that the use of swimming equipment gives an idea for something to do on dry land, or vice versa.

Equipment use changes over time with the experience of swimmers. The early years are for teaching swimmers to use equipment, why it is useful, and how it is designed for use. Later is the exercise of using it and still later is the use of those lessons and exercise to sophisticate equipment use.

The head coach needs to be sure that assistant coaches are using equipment according to their philosophy for use and to the ultimate plan as swimmers mature through the program.

For safety, it should be understood that equipment used in the water, if used to achieve physiological objectives, is likely to place certain stress on the muscle groups of swimmers. Just as there is wisdom in using cycles of exercise for dry land programming, there is also wisdom in using cycles of use with equipment in the water. For example, when equipment was scheduled for morning sessions as I described, over some 25 years of my career, we used that equipment on Monday, Wednesday, and Friday mornings, and we did not (typically) use the same equipment the same way at any other sessions.

The coach should be some and/or all of the following when leading practice with equipment:

- Creative: use of one item of equipment can often be a "lead up" or "follow up" to other items of equipment. That is, using certain items can lead to objectives achieved with other practice experiences. For example, sprinting after swimming with parachutes feels fast and light.

- Instructive: be observant for stroke flaws, as swimmers will tend to muscle through movement when they are trying to overcome resistance. They will often use instinct which may be counter-productive.

- Inspirational/motivating: when the coach is inspiring and motivating, it often grows into the group, encouraging team spirit. Often swimmers will achieve results they did not perceive to be possible by the use of equipment. Help them to believe!

- Summarizer: summarize the achievements of the practice so swimmers have understanding of the objectives and the accomplishments.

Finally, for the club coach, introduce equipment gradually and progressively. Teach the proper use of equipment, allow swimmers time to perfect its use and allow them to graduate from certain types of equipment to other types of equipment. Plan its use over the years they will participate in the program and according to their physical/mental readiness. Enjoy the results.

Paddles: the primary objectives are to use hand placement, progressive acceleration of hand speed, and proper exit from the water to keep the paddles firmly against the hands throughout the stroke cycle. They provide resistance as well, particularly larger paddles.

Fist Gloves: These are used to make a truly closed fist, and to remove feel for the water on the hands. When the gloves are removed from the hands, feel for the water is enhanced. Fist gloves are formed like mittens and made of something like thin rubber material.

Pull Buoy (at Hips and at Ankles): there are two categories of pull buoys. One is placed at the hips and more normal to see in use. The other is made by Finis and is placed at the ankles (typically). When placed at the ankles while pulling, the Finis buoys allows the hips to rotate more freely, and to achieve better horizontal lines during movement.

Bonus: The Finis buoy can be used for kicking by placing the wrists into the holes of the buoy.

Strap (D Band): straps are usually homemade by cutting inner tubes and using a figure 8 placement at the ankles. D Bands were introduced to the market by a great 400 IM swimmer from Puerto Rico and coach named Jesse Vassallo. D Band is a strong rubberized and circular band which fits tightly onto the ankles. Straps and D Bands are often used with pull buoys but can be used without buoys for greater resistance while swimming. Training with this equipment strengthens the upper body, helps swimmers to overcome neurological inhibition, and to feel the water. However, if used for training in longer sets or over-distance swimming it can be stressful to shoulders and should be cycled for planning purposes.

Pull Tube: these are small inner tubes that are also placed at the ankles for stabilization of the legs. They are used less than in previous years but can be used effectively for resistance or for stroke enhancement if they can be found.

Drag Suit: made similar to a male swimsuit but with 4 pockets surrounding the suit. They are usually used for resistance training.

Parachute: these are belts secured around the waste with a fabric tail and a parachute attached to the tail. Parachutes vary in two sizes. They are used for resistance training and to overcome neurological inhibition.

Surgical Tubing: this is very effective training material on several levels. It can be obtained at various thicknesses for greater or lesser resistance. My method for using it was to tie a rope through pool eyelets made for lane lines, tie surgical tubing to the rope, and use scuba belts to attach the tubing to the swimmer{s}. The rope through the eyelets was used for safety. Occasionally, tubing can deteriorate over time and break or it can slip at the belt attachment to the swimmer. It is better for the tubing to travel back through water than to travel back through air. As swimmers progress away from the wall, they are resisted as they approach the far wall, and when they return, their speed is assisted.

Weight Baskets and Weight Towers: these are gym baskets into which free weights are placed. Rope is tied to the basket placed on the pool deck, run through a pulley in a roof rafter, or some tight lane line cable run between poles > through the pulley high and back to a pulley at water level > to the swimmer and attached to the swimmer with a belt. The swimmer swims away from the wall and lifts the weight basket, which has free weights inserted into the basket. The swimmer typically swims in place against the resistance of the weight. Weight Towers can be purchased and used in much the same way but the Towers can be costly.

Buckets: this invention is from a great Florida coach named Randy Reese. Buckets are a VERY effective form of training equipment. Water is placed into buckets for weight resistance. A pulley system of fine but durable rope is used to allow the swimmer to achieve any pool distance. The rope is attached to the swimmer with a belt, and the swimmer pulls the Bucket upward, until they reach the other end of the pool. It is a very sophisticated form of resistance training.

<u>Fins</u>: fins are wonderful! They can be used with very novice swimmers and with very experienced swimmers for teaching stroke balance, stroke length, core body rotation, timing, and kicking. They can be used for speed assisted training. They can be used for underwater training and skill development. Swimmers usually like to use them. There are many fin types which can be used in various ways, depending on objectives.

<u>Clothes and Shoes</u>: I have used these items and I know they are used by some coaches; however, there are some reasonable considerations for their use. Shirts should have the sleeves cut out at the shoulders to allow free movement. Shirts and pants/shorts should be of light weight. Shoes can be problematic in that they can cause ankle and Achilles discomfort. I would encourage tight fitting socks as opposed to shoes or some type of water shoe. These items can be used for resistance and also to enhance kinesthetic awareness when the clothes are removed.

<u>Scuba Weight Belts</u>: these are good to use when vertical kicking in deep water. Vertical kicking is wonderful to help swimmers feel the requirement for using tops and bottoms of feet in the kicking motion. It is also good for breaststroke kicking, to feel foot placement, and the difference between a full range of motion and a partial range of motion.

<u>Vertical Kicking with Free Weights</u>: this vertical kicking is accomplished while holding onto free weights. Arms are involved, of course, and greater amounts of weight are possible.

<u>Wall Kicking</u>: this is great for breaststroke kicking to feel the effects of a full range of motion, feet acceleration and feet recovery pathway. Of course, they can also feel the forward thrust as hand pressure against the wall.

<u>Suits</u>: back in the day, swimmers used multiple suits in training to provide greater resistance during training. It was "a thing" to wear

out training suits, purchase a new one but keep wearing the older one over it until it was 2 or more suits. Girls and boys. Nowadays, tech suits have come to the sport and swimmers/coaches sometimes use them in training to achieve greater speeds than they can achieve in regular training suits.

There is probably training equipment that I have not included. I have used all of those mentioned at one time or another in my career. I recently saw a resistance mechanism that simulated the resistance of buckets—which involved a sophisticated pulley system and tall buckets in which the water is used to provide weight in the buckets for resistance—with a small device and tethers which provide a similar resistance. It was intriguing to watch, and I feel certain that coaches and swimmers will continue to invent future ideas for equipment use.

7 — A Better Athlete Makes a Better Swimmer

Most club teams have "dry land" programs for their swimmers. As coaches plan for exercise on dry land, the intent is always to help swimmers to be faster at racing in water.

The first question is whether to plan exercises that are specific to swimming movement, or to plan in a more general way with the goal of developing overall athleticism.

Either can be, and are, effective of course. Most coaches probably use some hybrid of the two philosophies for training swimmers on dry land. However, at some early stage of my career I made the choice for overall athleticism over specificity, based on the following points of logic:

1. Local schools were beginning to compromise their physical education programs by reducing classes (in some cases taking it out for entire years), using gyms for school assemblies and disrespecting physical education curriculum. Thus, there is less opportunity for development of "the athlete" in every child. Specific to the development of *mind<>body<>spirit* as equal elements of an ideal person, the body continues to be reduced in importance.

2. I decided that swimmers would experience specificity during their swimming.

3. I decided that a better overall athlete would make a faster swimmer.

4. I noticed that swimmers who came to the program with experience in gymnastics seemed more coordinated and stronger than others who had not experienced gymnastics; therefore, they often advanced more quickly in their swimming groups.

Today, I am even more convinced that general athleticism is a good strategy for club coaches. In addition to the previously mentioned rationale, children play less overall. They choose video games and are connected to cell phones over outside play or sports.

It became my goal to have a dry land program from entry level onto the swim team until graduation. Time allotments for dry land exercises gradually increased as swimmers advanced and aged through practice groups. Throughout the years, swimmers would increase from 20 minutes to 30 minutes, before eventually reaching a full hour of dry land practice.

Exercises at the earliest stage were concentrated on coordinated movement, eye-hand coordination, learning some basic calisthenics, attention to body/kinesthetic awareness as in body lines, flexibility, balance, and the effect(s) of the core body in movement. A topic of learning would often culminate with games or races.

Calisthenics are very important to the next stage of dry land. Calisthenics are simply using the resistance of body weight to achieve prescribed movement(s). Most people associate certain exercises with calisthenics such as push-ups, sit-ups, squat thrusts, pull-ups, planks, and lunges. But I also include flexibility and certain mobility exercises at this stage to give attention to range of motion.

I also think that some yoga exercises are very good at this stage of development. Examples of yoga exercises used are downward dog and child's pose for lower back, spinal twist for total body stretching, the tree for balance, plank for core strength, single arm side plank for arm and core strength plus balance, and head circles for neck mobility. Also the lotus, the cobra, the locust, and the bow (and variations) are yoga positions used for balance, flexibility, and strength. We didn't necessarily call them yoga exercises or use the names of them regularly. We just inserted the movement into the overall presentation of dry land exercise.

The last stage of dry land begins to use more equipment such as medicine balls, bands, and free weights (dumbbells specifically).

Specific to weights, I made the decision to keep maximum resistance at body weight or less. This decision was made because high school aged swimmers have yet to mature physically (or mentally); therefore, they are more susceptible to injury using heavy resistance. And – this allows for another level of development for the post high school years, when their bodies and minds are ready.

Throughout these stages of development, jump ropes were used continuously. While the investment in jump ropes is high as swimmers break them on an exponential scale, jump roping is an EXCELLENT exercise for aerobic development, muscular endurance, and coordination. Weighted jump ropes in combination with non-weighted jump ropes are wonderful.

The norm for scheduling dry land has always been 3 days per week, with a day between without dry land.

My objectives for the dry land program are always:

1. Teach fundamental safety specific to base of support, appropriate speed/acceleration of movement, concentric/eccentric phases of muscular contraction, range of motion, concentration

2. Enhance kinesthetic awareness

3. Improve muscular endurance

4. Develop physical power

5. Develop strength by *overcoming neurological inhibition* – this is strength development that is different from strength as related to increased muscle mass. Increased muscle mass is accomplished with high resistance and low repetitions. The development of muscle mass seems impossible for the club

swimmer who experiences such high repetition numbers in the water and out, during a typical day and 6 days per week of exercise. To *overcome neurological inhibition* on dry land, it is necessary, in our program, to exercise muscle groups to some level of fatigue – and continue to work for some repetitions beyond that point.

The next set of priority decisions to make is:

1. Determining how many sets and repetitions of exercises are necessary

2. Creating a plan for upper body, core body, and lower body development

3. Determining how to balance the development of opposing muscle groups (such as biceps and triceps, quadriceps and hamstrings, abdominals and lower back)

Competitive swimmers in USA club teams are normally categorized according to three broad categories. Those are

1. Novice - mostly 10 years of age and younger

2. Age Group - mostly 11 years to high school

3. Senior - which is normally defined by age (*late middle school to early high school*) and/or achievement levels of competition: that is state, regional, national, or international (where age groups are not (generally) relevant because competitions are based on qualifying times and seeding).

Novice swimmers are learning about movement and exercise. Time spent in dry land sessions should be limited, especially because attention spans at novice ages are often relatively short for exercise. Typically, while coaches and parents want improvement for children at these ages, swimmers are more focused on fun and enjoyment from their experience.

One set of exercise or movement and a number of repetitions should be enough for swimmers to practice and learn the movement(s) but not so many as to allow proper movement(s) to deteriorate respective to proper form and fundamentals to insure safety. Ten (10) repetitions is a good number for most exercises.

Age Group swimmers are ready for advancement. Exercises can be increased to three (3) sets and as many as twenty-five (25) repetitions, depending on the difficulty of the exercise and the collective maturity of the training group.

For senior swimmers, sets and repetitions depend on the objectives that the coach has for the exercise. When using equipment, this will be different for partner medicine ball use than it would be for butterflies using dumbbells.

It is at the senior level of the dry land program at which I want swimmers to *overcome neurological inhibition*. I want to *overcome neurological inhibition* by practicing excellent form when the muscle group is fatigued. This means that the resistance and the number of repetitions should be enough to cause some fatigue to that specific muscle group. It is normal for an athlete to compromise form in the exercise, specific to:

- Range of motion,

- Speed of the exercise

- The negative contraction of the exercise, and/or

- Breath.

Now, the coach must require excellence in movement from the swimmer at this point in time.

As examples:

1. Push-ups – As fatigue occurs, primarily in triceps and

pectoralis major muscle groups, athletes will often fail to exercise through a full range of motion, the speed of the movement often changes, and the head position tends to drop toward the floor. This may happen within 10 repetitions or 25 repetitions or 50 repetitions depending on the athlete. Regardless, the athlete needs to get to this point and maintain proper form for some number of repetitions to *overcome neurological inhibition.* The number of repetitions in excellent form beyond the state of fatigue is specific to the athlete also. It might be one or five or more.

2. Pull-ups – This exercise is difficult for many, even to accomplish one proper repetition. The difficulty is range of motion. The exercise is properly accomplished from a full hanging extension until the chin clears the pull up bar. To return to full extension and repeat the exercise is hard to do. But it is when this is fully accomplished that the athlete *overcomes neurological inhibition.* Spotting or band assistance can help with form on this exercise. Overhand grip is a different exercise from underhand grip: therefore, different muscle groups are exercised respectively.

3. Medicine Ball tosses – Concentration is necessary to catch the ball, bring the ball to the chest, sight to aim the throw, use progressive hand speed in the throw, and to follow through toward the target. When fatigued, these fundamentals are often compromised. The weight of the medicine ball determines how soon a compromise in fundamentals tends to happen. Athletes must achieve 100% good throwing fundamentals when fatigued to *overcome neurological inhibition.*

4. Overhead Triceps Extension with Dumbbell while lying face up on a bench – This exercise is designed to happen in a vertical line from behind the head, shoulders, and bench. Extension from the bottom portion of the movement will depend on the shoulder flexibility of the swimmer. It should happen with progressive hand speed and the follow through

of the movement should be to full extension of hands. The exercise should NOT bring the weight over the face or chest of the athlete. The movement should return to the lower point of extension in a full range of motion. That is dependent on the shoulder flexibility of the swimmer. The compromise of movement which is typical in fatigue is range of motion.

Now, if there is compromise in the form of the movement from the beginning of the set, the resistance is too heavy. If the athlete is not challenged with form by the end of the set, the resistance is not enough.

All of us have "comfort zones;" in these matters. It may take numerous sets to reach a fatigued state for an exercise. Athletes strengthen over time also; therefore, they must choose different resistance when they fail to experience fatigue in the exercise – if it is the goal to overcome neurological inhibition.

It is important to understand that the goal is not to fail in the exercise from fatigue. The objective is to maintain excellent form when it is uncomfortable to do so. One can overcome neurological inhibition when failure starts to occur; however, failure is a negative experience and one should not be in a state of failure on any regular basis.

For planning purposes, I like to use training circuits and I like to plan for upper body exercises, core body exercises and lower body exercises done in rounds of three. If the group can accomplish a round of three in 20 minutes, then three rounds are completed in an hour.

Generally speaking, physiological adaptation to an overload begins to happen in about 3 weeks and is usually completed in 6 weeks. Therefore, it is safe to add overload after a regimen has been exercised for 6 weeks.

Our swimming year is usually broken into three seasons: September through early December, late December through March/early April, late April through mid-August.

For Novice and Age Group swimmers, we normally take a week (7 days) off from dry land before the culminating meets in December.

For senior swimmers, we allot 10 days to 2 weeks off from dry land before culminating meets in December. Note: *We do like to continue with some abdominal exercise and flexibility/mobility exercise until a few days before the culminating meet, depending on the individual swimmer.*

Since 2005, for senior swimmers, early February would start a peak performance stage of the short course season. Peak performance started in late June for the long course season. As described in earlier chapters, peak performance refers to race specific, high intensity— high speed, intent to *overcome neurological inhibition*—swimming with speed to recovery ratios of at least 1:1 in the beginning phase of peak performance, and more recovery as the culminating meet(s) came closer in time.

During the short course, peak performance meets can include many championship experiences between late February and early April. Those are: state club regional championships, high school championships at regional and state levels, club state championships, and national championships.

During the long course season, peak performance meets include only club championships since high school swimming does not occur during long course months. Other long course championships in summer are regionals, states, zone, and national championships.

All championship meets are important to swimmers. Coaches are faced with a hard question relating to this circumstance. Does the coach "swim through" meets to focus on one meet in which to perform at the peak of the athlete's capabilities. Or, is there a way to perform at peak levels for all of the championship meets, because all of the championship meets are important to swimmers?

My decision on this question came to enter into a peak performance stage, or phase, of the season which would last for the duration of championship weeks. Swimmers' readiness for the peak performance stage is dependent on providing an excellent training foundation of aerobic and VO2max experience during the weeks and months leading up to the peak performance stage, so that endurance would last for the athlete throughout peak performance weeks or months.

Then the formula for peak performance became to follow each peak performance meet with ½ of the days remaining between the previous peak performance meet and the next peak performance meet – back into full peak performance training; that is, dry land, and a full schedule of training sessions were expected at this time. Following ½ of the days of "training up," the schedule was abbreviated with eliminating dry land exercise and reducing training intensity/number of sessions for the remaining ½ of days. This same regimen is repeated following and entering each successive championship meet.

High school meets are not included in counting training days. We simply used high school meets as peak performance training sessions where swimmers would be in their fastest suits, shaved, and racing at extremely high intensity.

The foundational idea underlying the method of the peak performance stage of the season is that swimmers will *overcome neurological inhibition* as they progress through the stages of training and meets. Performance improvements may not be as great from meet to meet as they might be if they focused on one meet – but – performance times have the potential to improve greatly over the entire period of time. And – swimmers can enjoy being competitive at all of the championship meets.

To maintain endurance throughout the peak performance period, it is important to have established a good endurance background with aerobic and VO2 Max training in the weeks and months leading into peak performance—and to get back into full peak performance training for ½ of the days following each peak performance meet. Coaches can count the days from the last day of the next peak performance meet, the middle of the meet, or the beginning of the meet. Factors concerning this count will be whether swimmers have distance events, middle distance, or speed events at the end of the meet.

Peak performance training and meets keep athletes prepared physically, but also strengthens mental toughness.

Mental toughness is more than a "will to win." Mental toughness is all of the elements relating to intellect that the athlete uses during the time leading up to races, during races and following races. But mental toughness is also the elements of life that one can eliminate from race consciousness at the time of the race, especially in peak performance times.

The Chinese philosopher Wu Men said it best,
"If your mind is not clouded with unnecessary things, this is the best season of your life."

This is done best when preparation has been excellent.

8 — Deliberate Practice

"Begin with the end in mind." - Dr. Stephen Covey, The Seven Habits of Highly Successful People

This statement is at the foundation of deliberate practice – and any other goal-centric endeavor. It is more than simply saying to oneself, "I want to be fast," or "I want to win the state championship," or "I want to make the Olympic Team." While those are goals that may or may not be reachable, they do define an end that gives direction.

The operative meaning though, answers numerous questions for the athlete, depending on their level(s) of experience. For example:

- How do I want to feel in the water?

- How do I want to split my race(s)?

- How do I want to use my energy?

- How do I want to apply my skills?

- How much strength and endurance will I need leading up to and including the end of the competition?

- How will I create that for myself?

- What "grit" will be required?

- How do I want my emotional state to be?

- How do I want to behave, regardless of the result, to be considered exemplary?

After one has imagined the "end of the journey," then one can play out the "ACTION" plan to achieve what has been imagined as the end. The action plan is the written commitment to oneself (and the support group) which gives the best possibilities for reaching the imagined end result(s).

For the age group swimmer, depending on their ages, the action plan is rather simplified. It can be stated in terms of goal times and split relationships, combined with specific practice habits.

For the senior level swimmers, especially between the ages of 14½ and 18+, life changes begin to happen. A mature coach will help those athletes navigate through many of the incidental factors which can affect the process but might not be easily anticipated. For example

Female athletes –

- Individual reactions to menstruation

- The importance (at these ages) of finding social groups that 'suit' the person

- Appearance and the perceived social importance of it respective to hair, makeup, clothes, etc.

- Academic/Athletic accomplishments and relevant perceptions

- Dating

Male athletes –

- The development of a social persona, possibly related to risk-taking, joking around, being loud, being quiet, athletic accomplishment, academic accomplishment, etc.

- Sometimes, the presentation of a seemingly standoffish personality

- Dating

All teenage athletes –

- As they age, teenagers want to "untether" themselves from the influence and reliance on adults such as parents, teachers, and coaches, and will gradually increase their own self-reliance and independence.

Altogether, teenagers have two driving forces which are necessary in their biological and psychological processes of becoming future adults.

1. The need to become independent

2. The need to be social beings (in some ways—which often times will be opposite from expectations of their relevant adults)

A wise coach should not (aggressively) resist, nor place significant moral judgment, on newly observed behaviors whether positive or negative. The coach should, however, advise whether behaviors are interruptive to the "action plan" for success. Therefore, my action plan was always to prioritize the elements of swimming in the following order:

DISCIPLINE- This is (possibly) the most important word to understand and live by than any other single idea or thought. It relates in early stages to imposed discipline; that is, the athlete accepts the rules which are placed on groups to establish certain behaviors in groups which elevate the possibilities for people in the group to achieve desired results, and for the group/team to achieve desired results.

When starting with a new team, or a new group, the coach has the responsibility of establishing discipline per their wishes for them to behave and perform accordingly. Eventually, as swimmers accept the imposed discipline as acceptable and/or necessary, they adapt to it and use it of their own volition; thus, they become self-disciplined, which is ideal. This process results in consistent behaviors which enhance the probability that they can be successful altogether.

Consistent behaviors are the results of discipline. Self-discipline is much stronger than imposed discipline. The coaches' goal should be to have groups of self-disciplined people.

GOALS – What will it take? – To win that state championship, to qualify for national championships, to make the Olympic Team, to win at the Olympics, or World Championships? These goals usually involve some research and some anticipation in terms of a predicted time that will be needed for achievement – or – possibly a race plan that may involve strategies to win races with specific and/or predicted opponents.

SPLITS – How does one want to race in that most important event? Does the swimmer want to get "out ahead" from the beginning of the race? Do they want to come from behind in the race? What is the plan for energy distribution in combination with the desired strategy? Practices should reflect planned race strategies. This item pertains specifically to the *Game of Racing*. It is important to relate to this factor, that it is the racing with other swimmers which is enjoyable and fun to do. Strategies and practice which provide the best opportunities for winning are for advancement of all competitors in the race, plus it is fun to "live out" your action plan with other worthy competitors. Pressure, anxiety, and fear are negative aspects of worrying about "what if I don't achieve?" Energy, eager anticipation, and confidence are positive aspects of hope about "what if I accomplish according to my plans?"

STRENGTH, MUSCULAR ENDURANCE, FLEXIBILITY – Once the swimmer's action plan is set, the coach needs to create a plan to maintain or increase strength capabilities, muscular endurance, and flexibility. Following that, the coach and swimmer need to communicate so that both understand the expectations and timeline.

SWIMMING SKILLS, ENDURANCE and SPEED – It is important to evaluate the time available from the start of the action plan until the "peak performance" competitions. This time frame will largely be different for each swimmer as their goals differentiate.

The **SAID** Principle – All of the prior elements of the action plan culminate in what is known as the SAID Principle. The SAID Principle says that **S**pecific **A**daptation to **I**mposed **D**emands starts (early stages) at three weeks and tends to reach maximum adaptation at about six weeks.

This means that after six weeks, it is suggested that newly imposed demands should be introduced, assuming another adaptation period is available.

Imposed demands are specific to repetition times on intervals, faster intervals, resistance, greater yardage achieved during the practice sessions, timed racing on "up and outs," shorter recovery times, etc.

The coach MUST be very aware of adding the demands to athletes, knowing times and racing qualities of swimmers, observing the effects of the training overloads on swimmers, and the adaptations which swimmers demonstrate in their practice performances, or not. These must be seen on a group basis, but also on an individual basis.

REST, RECOVERY, AND SPEED to ACHIEVE PEAK PERFORMANCE – Rest and Recovery are simply related to the idea of reducing the strain of physical training to levels where the athlete will realize more physical energy and a general well-being.

SPEED improvement is the physiological GOAL at this time though. Yardage amounts are naturally reduced as more rest and recovery is provided between repetitions which allows swimmers to perform with greater speeds. Dry land exercise is often adapted at this time as well. The coach and the athlete want to "*overcome neurological inhibition*" during this training time period, such that the BEST results can come at the BEST time(s). To *overcome neurological inhibition* is to swim at speeds faster than the nervous system allows, normally. To *overcome neurological inhibition* is to elevate performance past the nature of the nervous system to accomplish work—outside of its comfort zone.

Examples of people who overcome neurological inhibition are:

- As in an emergency situation when one accomplishes a feat of strength and/or endurance greater than "normal," such as lifting a car or a tree trunk off of someone,

- In weight lifting, it is not unusual for a person to fail at an attempt to lift a weight, then take several minutes to contemplate the task, and then be able to lift it. In this case, the person did not become stronger in that time of contemplation. They *overcome neurological inhibition.*

This concept is accomplished in training by swimming faster than predicted race speed(s) in preparation for the event(s). This can be accomplished in numerous ways:

Broken Swims – where the total distance is "broken" into shorter sections with short rest between which allows the swimmer to be faster than the predicted speed of the goal swim. It is usual for the sum of the broken swims to be equal to or faster than the goal time.

Use of swim fins can make swimming faster than normal.

Tethering the swimmer with surgical tubing, and timing the distance of the return swim when the tubing is assisting the speed of the swimmer. Neurological inhibition can be overcome also as the swimmer overcomes the resistance of surgical tubing to reach a wall.

Methods to *overcome neurological inhibition* are according to the creativity and ideas of the coach or swimmer(s).

Visual awareness is an important concept for efficient movement. I can't count the number of times I would tell my swimmers, "*My eyes give my brain the information it needs to tell my body what to do.*" We use this quip to alert athletes to the importance of visual awareness while swimming and while swimming fast. When the eyes are FOCUSED on key moments in time, it can enhance timing and what we refer to as "flow" in movement. For example:

- In backstroke, we want the timing of hip movement to be synchronized with the <u>recovery</u> of the arm as it reaches the high point in the recovery. It is as the arm comes into the field of vision, while the head is in its ideal position for movement. The head/eyes are not anticipating the sight, but rather being aware as it passes through. This is also an acceleration point for the recovering arm, and for the pulling arm, as it reaches the point of greatest leverage on the water and follows through in the stroke. This also keeps the recovery in line with the body.

- In butterfly, we like the eyes to be aware of the head position as the swimmer extends the head/neck for the breath – and sees the water level. It keeps the swimmer from lifting too high for the breath, which affects the hips negatively.

- In breaststroke, we like the swimmer to be seeing downward and forward (about a 45 degree angle) as the arms recover, being aware of awesome hand-speed. The head should be in line with the spine as the swimmer is lifted by the in-sweep of the arms and hands for breath.

- In freestyle, the head is best positioned in line with the spine respective to kinesthetics; however, a slight rise of the head allows for significantly more visual awareness. It allows for better peripheral vision for awareness of the race circumstances, and it allows for awareness of the front quadrant of the stroke. A slight forward tilt of the chin or otherwise lift of the head will not sacrifice rotation in the stroke mechanics, but it will allow for better visual awareness.

Focus of the eyes should be clear and alert to provide the brain with information it needs to tell the body what to do in the movement.

Direct visual awareness and peripheral visual awareness are important elements for the swimmer.

Direct visual awareness allows the swimmer to affect technical elements mostly. Peripheral vision is useful mostly with racing; that is, the swimmer can be aware of the race in the adjacent lanes.

It always surprises me when a swimmer says: "I didn't even know they were there." I know some swimmers want to "swim their own race" without regard to the lanes adjacent to them: however, that sometimes leads to losses simply because the swimmer was unaware. At least, if one has awareness, one can respond if need be. This is not to say that one needs to be directly focused on the adjacent racing circumstances such that they are swimming another's race, but it is good to keep visual awareness as one moves. "*The eyes give the brain the information it needs to tell the body what to do.*"

The best 'exposé' that I have read on the subject of visual awareness is: *The Inner Game of Tennis: The Classic Guide to the Mental Side of Peak Performance* by W. Timothy Gallwey.

This book gives attention to "the mental game" as its primary thesis, but it is also great on the subject of using visual clarity and focus to be better at movement. Gallwey offers examples of seeing not only the ball in tennis and baseball, but seeing the threads on the ball as it comes toward you.

I don't know why, but many swimmers swim as if they are almost blind; that is, without focused visual awareness of what is happening as they move.

Deliberate Practice means we must "begin with the end in mind." *To begin with the end in mind, one should actually visualize the realization of the goal(s).* And – they should imagine their behavior at the moment of the realization of the goal(s).

Think it through, not only for the result, but for the way that the swimmer will "carry themselves" so to speak. It is natural and understandable to be elated and to show that elation; however, athletes should be careful not to diminish the accomplishments of others in that moment of elation. It is an element of good sportsmanship to respect the fact that all people who are engaged in the event are there for you. Without them, you might not have been able to achieve the realization of your goal.

Therefore, it seems inappropriate to demonstrate dominance over another competitor or competitors by pounding water with fists, yelling to express dominance, or making facial expressions which elevates oneself while (possibly) diminishing others. It is sometimes natural to do these behaviors, especially if rivalry is at hand between individual athletes or countries, but it is probably true that the win might not be possible without the competition; therefore, the competition is to be respected.

To begin with the end in mind and to create action plans are intellectual processes. Then, the objective is for the coach and the athlete to be altogether in the moment during all levels of preparation. This ability to communicate and collaborate is an important life skill development.

Learn to compartmentalize your consciousness.

For teenagers, whose lives are "bombarded" with changing variables, there is a tendency to overlap their thoughts on everything.

But, one cannot, or should not, try to control academic considerations while at athletic practice, nor can they control their weekend plans while in chemistry class, and so on. To the extent that they can learn to put their full consciousness on the "thing" they are doing at the moment they are in, they can elevate that "thing" to higher performance.

So, don't think about homework while you are at practice and don't think about the weekend while you are in an academic class. Rather, give total concentration to each of those matters when you are involved in them – totally!

Compartmentalization is a major factor relating to discipline. It is when consciousness tends to overlap, discipline is compromised. The quality of skill development, physiological adaptations, and positive spirit associated with the practice will be best when consciousness is in the moment.

Another example of overlap is when athletes think about the end result before giving attention to the process of the race itself. The result can provide motivation to give a hard effort; however, it can create nervousness, and an inability to perform in the race according to skills actualized and race strategy performed appropriately.

While it is true that ideal performance is often achieved in a state of "no mind" or "*Mushin*," when preparation has happened with total consciousness during the process for a sufficient time, to put the desired result ahead of performance while doing it, to put the result outside of a reasonable perspective, will more often interfere with ideal performance.

Altogether, getting from the point where one has begun with the end in mind, to the point of realizing that end, is simple; that is, imagine it, create an action plan, live the action plan, and realize the result.

It is simple, but not easy to do.

The athlete is in a daily conflict with instinct and human nature to overcome interfering thoughts and emotions, which can interrupt the process.

Sickness or injury can also interfere with the process as well. But perspective and reasonable action(s) can accommodate for these instances in most or many circumstances.

Finally, on these matters, time is often a factor. The athlete and the coach need to allow the time necessary to achieve. For example, it may be that a goal has been planned to happen within a season, but the athlete is not ready at that particular time. It is important to understand that the goal is to provide motivation for the process. It sometimes happens that the goal is not achievable within the time frame available. The goal should continue to motivate the athlete because it is the process, or the journey, which strengthens the individual character of the person.

I once knew a swimmer who placed 3rd at three consecutive Olympic Trials meets. She trained for 12 years in hopes of making the USA Olympic Team in IM races, but she never made the team. She became an enormously successful person in her life following her training years, using much of what she experienced in her journey as an athlete to drive successes in her career and her personal life.

So—be the best you can be in your journey and believe in yourself, your coaches, and your beliefs as good guides to advance your life experiences.

9 — Swimmers' Points of View

Club swimmers, especially during teen years, often think in and make statements in "all or none" terms. They might just be overstatements. Or, maybe they simply sense time in different ways from reality.

Regardless, this chapter is an attempt to give coaches ways of providing needed perspective to swimmers.

I have often heard swimmers, when describing their daily schedule or their training state: "I train every day at 4:30 a.m. and I have to wake up by 4:00 a.m. every, day and I come back every day and train for 2 to 3 additional hours in the afternoon—year-round." There is probably some truth in the statement: however, it is not entirely true. Statements such as these can form false realities for swimming which can cause unneeded stress. These types of statements normally happen in interviews, when talking with other swimmers or people who ask about their training. They can also cause misunderstandings for whomever is hearing the statement.

Stated truthfully and correctly, the statement should be:
"I train double sessions three times per week during the most demanding part of the season, usually about 6 to 12 weeks. We always build up to the most demanding part of the season, and we adapt the training to fewer sessions and fewer hard days following the most demanding training. We usually divide the year into three seasons so there are 3 time periods in the year when the training is demanding on my time. Each week we are off on Saturday evening and all day Sundays."

Said the first way, the difficulty and "sacrifice" seem undoable. Said the second way, the statement is exactly true, and while the difficulty is significant and a "hard thing," it is not seemingly undoable or unworthy of doing.

Another statement is: "I don't have a social life," when there are actually a great many opportunities to be social as an athlete. The team settings in practices and meets are social, traveling to competitions in and out of state are social opportunities, getting together with schoolmates on weekends is social, family events are social, etc. What should not be done, which many non-athletes consider to be social, are parties with drinking or drugs which alter consciousness.

Whitney Hedgepeth stated it well after she took a training break following the 1988 Olympics. Whitney started training again in November 1988 after being in Seoul, Korea, in September. She spoke to the team about her experience altogether and said the following (paraphrased): "I always thought I was missing 'stuff' because of my training schedules. Now I have been off of training for 2 months and I realize I wasn't missing anything special. It seems like everybody is just riding from the Burger King at one end of the boulevard to the McDonald's at the other end of the boulevard until we all go home for the night. Swimming enabled me to meet and interact with people all over the country and even in a handful of foreign countries, culminating with the Olympics, which is the biggest healthy party ever. I would choose my social life in swimming versus the social life I thought I was missing. I missed y'all while I wasn't swimming."

Oftentimes, it seems like swimmers perceive a season to be a year. Swimmers will often say: "I did that 3 years ago and I haven't done it since." More often than not, the time period was probably 3 seasons.

But, because of the newness of training, they are likely to articulate the statement out of context.

For example, consider a circumstance where a pool has currents which affect the outside lanes; that is, lane 1 is against the current and lane 8 is with the current. Lane 1 is likely to swim significantly slower than their best time and lane 8 is likely to swim significantly faster than their best time. Lane 1 might claim they are getting slower while lane 8 is elated—but might have trouble getting back to the current assisted time. It may take the swimmer in the current assisted lane several seasons to swim faster. The truth is that both swimmers gave their best effort which is a positive factor, yet each swimmer has a false perception of the circumstance – unless they are informed as to the circumstance and keep a reasonable perspective about the event. It is not unusual for the swimmer to say they did the faster time "years ago" when it has actually been seasons.

Given there are 3 seasons in a typical year, the swimmer sometimes perceives them as years.

As stated earlier, it is not abnormal for teen swimmers to experience "plateaus" as physiologies and psychologies change. The key to success is to stay positive and perceive every practice and every meet as an opportunity to prepare to be the best you can be. This approach allows swimmers to experience the best opportunities for improvement.

It is good and valuable to do hard things. This is a true statement. Consciousness is, more often than not, changed for the better when a person overcomes a hard challenge and is strengthened by the experience.

But it seems like it is not enough to experience situations in terms of hard or easy. I think the worst place to be, and the place where swimmers often find themselves is "in-between." This is when the swimmer is trying pretty hard (comparatively), but not at their best. It is possible to feel fatigue after every practice in a season while one fails to accomplish the repetition speeds necessary to achieve the goals of the swimmer. In this circumstance, the swimmer will likely fall short of their goal(s) and say they practiced hard "for nothing." The truth is they were "in-between" which caused a failure to adapt to efforts with relevant speed(s) to achieve the goal(s).

For example: imagine that a swimmer is capable of being under 1:00 on 10 x 100 yards freestyle on 1:15 but she is going 1:02+ on them. Her heart rate is at 170. Her teammate beside her is going 1:02 also. Her breath is labored. Her stroke count is 15 strokes per length. It seems like she is good on the set, but still, she could repeat under 1:00. She just needs to increase her stroke rate slightly. She is in-between. Her performance on the set may keep her from getting slower, but it will not necessarily help her to be faster. When she needs to hold 1:00s in a 1,000 yard freestyle race, she may not be able to because she was "in-between" on the practice set(s).

It has been rare in my experience where one who is "in-between" has met hard objectives. And – it is frustrating because the person thinks they are "pretty good" in practice but they are not getting faster. The affected swimmer can, and will (normally), compare to someone else who might be slower on repetitions but faster in the event. This can happen if the person who was slower was (typically) swimming their fastest possible in the set; that is, that girl who was swimming 1:02 beside her was out of her comfort zone to do so. She may be the one who achieves.

An in-between attitude about "things" is frustrating because it often gives the "illusion" that one deserves more for trying but is not rewarded because it was not enough.

People can be in-between and be fast between the flags, but too slow on turns, or fail to perform a correct number of dolphin kicks underwater, or glide in on the finish, etc. Maybe you should be racing with someone faster but you chose a "less competitive" person to race on the set. It is possible to leave the practice and feel tired, even if you have not been at your best effort for the day.

The swimmer might say, "I try hard every day but I have not improved my times."

Normally, a good axiom is to be out of your "comfort zone" when asked to be so by your coaches; that is, really *try your best to be your best*, including all technical elements.

On another level, imagine the coach has asked the male swimmers to be under 30 strokes per length and repeat under 2:10 for 5 x 200 meter freestyle repetitions on 3:00. This means the swimmer must be exceptionally core driven, extend to his full length with the recovering arm, follow through on the pulling arm with progressive hand speed, kick with a strong 6 beat kick to maintain a fully horizontal body line, and build effort over the distance of the repetitions, do the appropriate number of dolphin kicks underwater while in a perfect streamline, and finish well to the wall—on every repetition. This challenge is as much mental as it is physical. The athlete should not be in-between on it.

Most people (actually) train at in-between levels most of the time; that is, they give a good effort, but not necessarily effort which changes them physiologically, or psychologically, or emotionally. This is at the core of the reality which is called a plateau in most circumstances.

In-between is to compromise the ideal. On its face, one can see the problem with it.

The lifestyle of USAS Club competitive swimmers is indeed special for high school-aged "kids." For swimmers who train and compete at a senior level for four years, swimming consciousness will (most likely) be all they will need, or want to be competitive at their chosen levels after high school. This is because their high school schedules are more challenging. Typically, they start many days between 4:00 and 5:00 a.m. They practice for 90 minutes to two hours and then go to school for 7 hours. They return to an afternoon training session of 2 to 3 hours. They have dry land exercise at least 3 times per week. They do this Monday through Saturday morning. They compete at least once per month and more at certain times in the season. Meets are 2½ days to 5 days of competition in (about) 9 to 15 events. They have homework at night and they normally compete well in their academics. They balance this with family life and whatever other activities they do outside of swimming. As stated earlier, this schedule is not 100% of the time, but it is for a significant time period in each season. They train and compete up and down with endurance and speed objectives – but it is a heck of a four-year schedule.

Collegiate swimming, masters swimming, and/or professional swimming will pale by comparison to club swimmers' daily schedules.

Keep in mind:

1. This schedule is *sometimes*, not all of the time, but it is a lifestyle nevertheless.

2. The coach is responsible to help the athlete stay out of the "in between" circumstance; that is to use whatever behavior is required for a given athlete. The coach needs to encourage with motivating language, call out times, and remind athletes when necessary, state improvements needed to improve times, and, even reprimand if needed. *Note: If an athlete is unresponsive, a separate meeting outside of practice might be required to help the athlete get back on course. The athlete could be dealing with problems outside of swimming. It might be a time to teach or remind the athlete about mental compartmentalization and/or perspective.*

3. It is often the case that swim meets or practice are too emotionally charged to be able to communicate effectively. If this is the case, schedule a separate time to discuss the matter. But—make sure that appropriate perspective is realized.

Some need significant help to navigate all that is happening in their lives during this time. It is primarily up to parents, teachers, and coaches to help them keep perspective and progress to great lives as adults.

Occasionally, matters can be, or can become, emotional. I have been in my share of emotional exchanges in 51 years of coaching. Looking in the rear view mirror, I cannot remember a single circumstance when I acted out a need to win an emotionally-charged interaction, that turned out to be to the benefit of anyone. Typically, it was worse for each of us involved plus the people around us. AND— perspective was more often lost altogether.

Regardless of age, the coach should always strive to demonstrate "adult" characteristics such that emotions are kept under control. That is not to say that the coach needs to compromise their "firm ground values"; however, try to do so with minimal emotion. This idea applies to demonstrations of elation, as well as demonstrations of disappointment.

Keep proper perspective!

10 — Nutrition? Good Question

There is the science of nutrition, and then there are my Mom's rules from when I was young:

- "I prepared the meal so clean your plate."

- "I give you all of the food groups every day. Clean your plate."

- "Everything in moderation. Don't overeat and don't under-eat. Clean your plate—once."

- "Don't eat junk snacks. If you do, you won't want to clean your plate later."

- "What you don't like is the best thing for you. What you like is the worst thing for you."

- "Finally, wash the dishes and make sure the plates are clean."

As a coach of 51 years, I have seen many trends:

- Carbohydrate loading

- Vegetarian diets, meat diets, selective fasting

- Caffeine to stimulate

- Low carbohydrate diets with high protein intake.

- Electrolyte drinks

- Protein shakes

- Creatine

- Chocolate milk

- Beet drinks and chews

As Jack Nelson stated on his club T-shirts: "The Body Can Achieve What the Mind Believes." I guess a case can be made for all of that list in certain circumstances; however, club swimmers would do well to live by my Mom's rules. A balanced daily diet to include some things for which the athlete finds NOT to their liking—will fuel athletes consistently for their best performance. And, of course, don't forget to hydrate.

There is definitely science associated with nutrition and physiology. It may be that there is some physiological benefit to "things" that are promoted for performance enhancement; however, serious caution is recommended because:

- Money is the basic motivation for sales, so results might be exaggerated.

- If the athlete comes to believe it is necessary for performance, and then is without the enhancement, it might cause something along the scale of nervousness to anxiety, which can deter performance.

- Reliance on preparation is the best option since it is largely under the control of the athlete and the coach.

There are 3 Primary Principles for sports nutrition:

1. Fuelling using all of the food groups

Food Groups:

- Fruits & Vegetables - Benefits are vitamins and minerals

- Grains - Benefits are carbohydrates, protein, fiber, vitamins and minerals

- Protein Foods (meat, fish, eggs, soy) - They are necessary for muscle maintenance and building

- Dairy - The benefit is calcium (milk, yogurt) for bone/skeletal strength

- Fatty Foods (that is, healthy fats) - Monounsaturated (plant based oils, nuts, avocados, seeds) and Polyunsaturated Fats (flaxseeds, fish oil, sunflower oil, nuts) for general good health

A typical average caloric intake recommended for competitive swimmers is between 2,870 calories and 3,370 calories from the 5 food groups daily, whether involved in training or competition. This caloric intake is for competitive swimmers considering moderate to strenuous training sessions and swim meets.

Specifically, each athlete will need to determine their ideal caloric intake and estimate their typical caloric expenditure. It may change, particularly for club swimmers, as they move through puberty stages, add to their daily schedules with double training sessions, and school matriculation.

This can be accomplished by keeping nutritional logs, especially at periods of change in physiology and training. A normal body weight change will be within about 3 pounds. If larger weight swings in either direction are noticed over a week's time period, one should take notice and evaluate whether a change is recommended; that is, if a swing under normal body weight range occurs for a week of time, caloric intake should be increased. If a swing above normal weight range occurs, caloric intake should be reduced. However, if the athlete has realized a growth spurt, it will probably explain an increase in body weight range.

I lb. = 3500 calories

That is a good statistic of which to be aware. For example, if one adds 500 calories per day to their diet without a proportional caloric expenditure, a pound will be gained in a week. If one adds 1,000 calories per day to their diet, it reduces the time to add weight by half. Likewise, reduction of calories in the same amounts will have the same effect with weight loss.

The formula simplifies the matter significantly. There are plenty of fads and advertisements selling weight products and systems for weight control. Products may claim to produce an energy advantage. But—they are motivated by the inclination of many people to gain an easy advantage or change by easier methods than normal preparation.

The BEST method for weight control and energy enhancement is to be consistently disciplined to a well-balanced, natural diet—and to prepare with deliberate practice.

2. Hydration - **WATER IS BEST!**

Athletes can hydrate with (almost) any fluid, but water is simple, less expensive, and best for hydrating.

The more you tend to perspire, the more you need to hydrate. The more active you are, the more you need to hydrate.

- The body temperature and heart rate may rise when the total amount of water in the body is below the normal levels.

- One may feel more fatigued than usual when dehydrated.

- One may not think clearly. Motor control, decision-making abilities, and concentration may be impaired if dehydrated.

- The body's natural functions may slow down if dehydrated.

- Performance in sport or exercise may not be as good as it could be if dehydrated.

Therefore, plan and act. Take fluid, preferably water, during exercise sessions and meets. Electrolyte replacement may be needed and electrolyte drinks can accomplish it well. The most commonly measured electrolytes are: sodium, potassium, chloride, and bicarbonate. Electrolytes are reduced when sweating. Sweating might cause a greater need for an electrolyte drink during summer workouts or when indoor pool temperatures and/or water temperatures are high.

But be careful and use electrolyte drinks in moderation.

3. Recovery is necessary to restore an athlete's mind and body.

Replenish glycogen stores after long or intense workouts—The body burns carbohydrates that are stored in the muscle (glycogen). Eating carbohydrates will rebuild glycogen stores—½ gram per pound of body weight is a general guideline; that is, 75 grams for a 150 lb. person.

Repairing damaged muscle following long or intense workouts: Eating 20–40 grams of high quality, lean protein will assist protein synthesis to repair muscle and enhance muscle growth. If at a swim meet, swimmers may want to delay this much consumption of protein until the end of competition, particularly if the person's digestive system feels overly full or if digestion is considered difficult during competitive events.

Swim meets offer a challenging circumstance for many club swimmers; that is, the length of a single session can be as many as 6 plus hours. Swimmers might be scheduled for a warm up session as early as 6:30 a.m. and not be out of the competitive meet until after 1:00 p.m. If the meet is a preliminary—finals meet, they might be back at 4:00 p.m. for finals warm-up, and the competitive session might last until 9:00 p.m. I have experienced long course meets that started at 6 a.m. and ended after midnight—"back in the old days." Whatever the specifics of the particular meet, the following are good habits to develop for meets:

Breakfast - This is a VERY important meal in which to consume significant calories of carbohydrates and grains. And hydrate! It should be about 1,000 calories, plus or minus a couple of hundred. There will be some hunger from the previous day; there may be some nervousness for a new meet day. It will get the swimmer through warm-ups and likely the first event or more.

I understand, some swimmers do not like to eat a lot for breakfast. This is fine, but schedule breakfast consumption gradually during the early morning hours; that is, have something every 45 minutes to an hour which can be digested gradually. BUT DO NOT SKIP BREAKFAST! Hydrate with breakfast, during, and after warm up.

<u>Snack</u> - Mid-morning. (Bagel, yogurt, fruit, sandwich, energy bar, chocolate milk, energy shake or smoothie, etc.) This should be scheduled after a swim down from an event or before a warm up for an event. And hydrate!

<u>Lunch</u> - Scheduled at the pool if the session goes past noon or after the session. This should be a balanced meal; that is, all of the food groups should be consumed (ideally). Hydrate.

<u>Snack</u> - Mid-afternoon. Hydrate

and/or

<u>Pre-finals meal</u> - All food groups should be consumed (ideally). Hydrate.

<u>Snack</u> - During Finals if hungry but definitely hydrate.

Nutrition should be planned and adhered to according to the plan. A circumstance which often occurs for club athletes is that they get behind on their nutrition, putting them into a "caloric debt," from which it is difficult to catch up.

For example: Imagine that a swimmer skips breakfast on a day of training, but attends morning practice, has a sandwich for lunch, goes straight to practice after school, and picks up fast food for dinner after practice—all while forgetting to hydrate effectively throughout the day. Then, the next day will be making up for the bad day before, regardless of a better nutrition day following it. Given the amount of calories burned on the bad day, and the lack of hydration, it might take days of disciplined nutrition to make up for the one bad day.

If good nutritional habits are practiced in a disciplined fashion and caloric intake is balanced with caloric expenditure, body weight will be as it should be—and athletic performance will be reasonably good on that basis. The athlete will not need to worry about body weight, strength, or endurance.

"Empty" foods can be a problem. Chips, sweets like cakes and cookies, or other 'gut fillers,' are NOT caloric intake that will meet nutritional needs. They should be minimalized to special occasions or consumed in absolute moderation. For example, one might eat a small cup of ice cream daily but one should not eat a waffle cone with 3 scoops of ice cream daily—even in the summer.

Navigating Potential Nutritional Barriers -

1. Vegetarian/Vegan - These dietary preferences require significant research to develop a balanced diet for the athlete. They also require even greater discipline than other dietary preferences. At meets especially, swimmers should take food on the trip with them in the case they need to eat separately from the chosen restaurants for the team, or they need to take their personal food ingredients, such as cheese or dressing. A balance of carbohydrates, protein, vitamins and minerals, dairy (possibly soy milk), and healthy fats need to be in any special diet.

2. "I don't like that" - is the more common challenge for young people. The answer for athletes is to "acquire a taste for it" or to use a blender to make a shake of the foods or some other method to insure a balanced diet for training and for performance. All athletes must be educated as to the importance of balanced nutrition as it relates to training and athletic performance. As I stated earlier in this book, I was fortunate to attend a Military School. We were provided 3 balanced meals each day without options. Initially, the food

was NOT to my liking. Within 3 weeks I was hungry enough to accept it. I acquired tastes as needed. I have rarely had a problem with the taste of foods since I acquired tastes, as necessary, at that school.

3. "There is not enough time" - The key to this statement is to plan for time. Make proper use of time. It can be done. There are ways to accomplish behaviors which suit the needs of the athlete. Think it through because it is important! The analogy is often used, "You have to have gas in your car for it to run." (One might say electricity in the 21st century.) Regardless, the vehicle needs energy to run. The analogy is correct. Without energy provided by fuel, the body will fail.

4. For the club swimmer, much of the responsibility tends to fall on the parent(s). While this is true for most club swimmers, the club swimmer eventually ends up with the responsibility. The sooner they take ownership of planning for the need, the better prepared they are for their future successes.

The overall goal is for the club swimmer to be a Complete Athlete. Nutrition is often left to the inclinations of swimmers to do what they like. Unless they like preparation, hard things, competition, and ideal nutrition, they are likely to be incomplete according to what they don't like. As in all areas of training, club swimmers need to be disciplined to accept and practice good nutrition.

11 — Lessons Learned

"For the raindrop, joy is entering the river." – Ghalib

In 51 years of coaching, there have been thousands of swimmers, their families, coaches, and colleagues who have made it a coaching life. I would like to name every one, and state ways they impacted me in positive ways toward a successful career and a wonderful life. And there is no way to describe the many ways my own family sacrificed attention to them while I made the attempts to do "whatever it takes" to be "there" for the athletes I coached.

It is impossible to do that of course.

When starting the career, there were no indications as to what direction it would take, nor how I would navigate the obstacles I would confront. Now, the quote to start this chapter seems most appropriate. My joy has been to be in the river. It is to have experienced every person and every event as it happened.

When I think about it, Whitney Hedgepeth and Rada Owen made Olympic Teams. Many others made Olympic Trials, were champions on various levels, were wonderful swimming technicians, were outstanding trainers, were exceptional racers, were incredible people to know and with whom to work, were great assistants as coaches for teams, were special colleagues to know, and adopted as family members. There were awesome volunteers who were also wonderful parents.

Indeed, *I was the raindrop and the joy was entering the river.*

In this chapter, I would like to describe the places I worked and some lessons I learned from being there. My hope is that any of the people who were at those places will know they were extremely important to those lessons.

The Glendale Gators: Summer months 1968, 1972, 1973, 1974

This was my first paid coaching experience. In 1968, I was paid $5 added onto my lifeguard wage to assist Bill Nixon who was the head coach. I was 20 years old. Neither Bill, nor myself, were very knowledgeable about competitive swimming, but both of us were entirely enthused about coaching the team. Motivating swimmers was our mantra that summer. And swimmers responded by attending practices and racing their hearts out at the weekly swim meets. Glendale had moved up to "the A league" after being champions in "the B league" the previous summer. Therefore, we lost more meets than we won that summer. But you couldn't tell we were losing most of the time. The swimmers were entirely proud to race for their community and for each other. We had a great time every week! This was the first time (as a coach) that I realized the effect of a gleeful and positive esprit de corps in a team and for a community. Bill and I worked diligently to set up meet events each week so we would have the best chance to be as competitive as possible. The community supported the team and attended all meets to cheer them on to competitive efforts. The summer was, in a word—FUN! It was the beginning of something that I did not realize at the time. As the successive summers passed, I felt increasingly confident from courses in physical education during my time at Old Dominion University.

The Fort Bragg Aquadragons: September 1971 to September 1972

I was drafted into military service during that summer of 1968. Rather than enter into the draft. I joined the U.S Air Force for 4 years. I was an air to ground radio operator for most of my time in the Air Force. I was stationed in Panama from April 1970 until September of 1971. When I returned from Panama, I was placed into a Security Police group because radio operators were not needed in the United States at that time. While investigating vandalism at a colonel's house on Pope AFB, the Colonel shared that he had five children who swam for the Fort Bragg Aquadragons—and they needed an assistant coach. I told him I had been a swimmer and coached so I could do that job. He got me re-assigned to Army Special Services so I could coach the Aquadragons. Grant Maas was the head coach. He was a good man, and we worked well together. The swimmers were all children of Army Green Berets, and Airborne Troops, and Air Force children. They were naturally disciplined and they did practically everything given by Grant and me in a consistent way. We were focused on winning the league championship for the league we were in—and we did. That was a team of excellent trainers and dynamite racers. During that year, Grant and I also attended a coaching clinic with Doc Councilman (author of the *Science of Swimming*) and Peter Daland, the coach at University of Southern California. It was a very informative clinic. Both Grant and I felt more adept at coaching after the clinic. I also read *The Science of Swimming* cover to cover, and used it as a constant resource for many years. The swimmers and the parents of the Aquadragons were 100% supportive which made the time I spent with the swimmers and parents another positive factor in what would become a career in the future.

The Bounty Otters Swim Club: September 1974 to September 1977

In September 1973 I enrolled at Old Dominion University as a Health, Physical Education, and Recreation major with the intent of being a coach. I had a required swimming class. The ODU swim coach taught the class. He asked me to consider joining the swim team after observing me swim in the class. I agreed to join. After that year, Mary Fleet (a Hall of Fame swimmer at ODU) was selected to coach the ODU swim team. She knew I was coaching during the summers, and that I was older than all of the ODU team members, so she asked me to assist her in the start-up of a club team through the Bounty Outreach program at ODU. I agreed. She was merging a group of swimmers—with whom she was working—with a team from the Oceana Naval Base called the Ocean Otters. The resulting team was called the Bounty Otters Swim Club. The team had about 50 swimmers in that first year. Mary moved to California and a new coach was hired to coach ODU in 1975. He was assigned the responsibility of coaching BOSC also. Within a number of weeks, he delegated the responsibility to me. In September of 1975, BOSC grew some on its own, but another event also occurred. The Peninsula YMCA Swim Team (from Newport News, Virginia) folded. The Peninsula YMCA was coached by a good friend and colleague named John Ryan who moved to San Antonio, Texas, and became a legendary coach in that area. Since I was from Newport News, grew up swimming with John, had spent time in the service, and coached as he had, he recommended that the Peninsula YMCA swimmers join the BOSC. Many of them did and the team grew to about 150. Two wonderful assistants came to the rescue at the same time and helped tremendously with the novice and age group level swimmers. This exceptional combination of swimmers, their parents, and the coaching staff blended into a great team. BOSC won the short course Virginia Age Group Championship that year—for the first and only time. Two swimmers, Penny Shelor and Dan Naumann qualified for the AAU Junior National Championships. I had to learn about entering and participating in that level of competition for those swimmers. They attended the short course (Dallas, Texas) and long course (Gainesville, Florida) meets.

This year (September 1976 - September 1977) was extremely rewarding but also extremely stressful. I started my graduate studies in Athletic Administration. My son was 3 years-old and my wife worked as an elementary teacher. I was taking a class schedule which would allow me to graduate in one year. I was coaching 2 morning practices per week, every weekday afternoon, and Saturday mornings. I was writing a thesis; therefore, I was in the ODU library until 10 p.m. many nights. And I was commuting from Newport News to Norfolk daily. Finally, I was hoping to be hired to coach the ODU team but failed to get the job. Altogether, BOSC during 1976-77 was a year spent with people who engulfed my consciousness for the future. The end of it was emotional, rewarding, unforgettable, educational, and tiring to a degree I had never experienced before. I actually think that failure to be hired at ODU was a gift because I needed to balance the year I had experienced with some relief.

<u>*The Indian River Swim Team*</u> (Vero Beach). September 1977 to
June 1978

The balance I needed happened in Vero Beach, Florida. Since
ODU hired a coach from California, I attended the long course Junior
Nationals with a bag of resumés, and looking for a job as a club
coach. Within weeks I was hired by the new Indian River Community
College coach, Jim Montrella, to coach a division of the Indian River
club team which would be based at the Vero Beach YMCA. There was
already a division at the Ft. Pierce location, and new divisions were
to be started at Vero Beach and Stuart, Florida. I held tryouts for the
Vero Beach division. Almost all of the swimmers who tried out were
new to the sport. They came out in board shorts and bikinis. This was
a group that I would start from scratch as competitive swimmers.
On the one hand, the challenge was great, but on the other hand, the
coaching time was much less than the previous year. In fact, I was
coaching 2 hours per day in the beginning and spent most of the
remaining days at the beach. It was the rest I needed to balance the
previous year. I was paid half of a salary by Indian River Community
College and half by the Vero Beach YMCA. I am so grateful for this
year. Jim Montrella, and his wife Bev, became lifelong friends. Jim
was a great mentor, a colleague and example of a good coaching life.
All of the swimmers were "game." They endured the early lessons of
swimming technique, discipline, training, and racing. They did not
ever quit at any of the tasks they were given. They improved in what
I would call quantum leaps from the first day until 10 months later.
They were always respectful. Their parents were always part of the
solution. None were ever part of the problem. I added to practice
expectations as they progressed and none of them ever resisted. I
loved coaching that group of swimmers from their beginning until
the day I moved back to Virginia. And—I liked Vero Beach as a place
to live. I liked it so much that I live in Vero Beach now.

Jim taught me some about owning a business too. He owned a
business called Modern Concepts. Jim invented hand paddles for
learning and training. I had used them with swimmers at BOSC and

I encouraged Vero Beach swimmers to buy them so we could use them. One day, Jim visited to watch a practice, and the swimmers were using the hand paddles. They had rubber finger straps and wrist straps. Jim shared the following story with me (paraphrased):

"Dudley, when I invented the hand paddles, I did not manufacture them with wrist bands. It was purposeful because if there was a stroke flaw it would show up, as the paddle would either change position on the hand(s), or it would come off from the hand(s). They were designed to improve technique, especially in freestyle and backstroke. Well, I kept hearing from coaches that they were drilling holes at the back so they could put wristbands on them—and use them to improve power in swimming strokes. So, to sell them, I put wristbands on them in manufacturing so they would sell better. [Then he suggested that I have swimmers remove the wristbands and use them for technique improvement.] When technique is improved, they won't need the wristbands to keep them on their hands, and they can be used for training in that way as well." I have never used wristbands on hand paddles since that day.

Jim and Bev are two of the people I have most respected in my coaching journey. And—I know this is felt by many others in competitive swimming also.

The Tritons of Petersburg (TOP)/The Virginia Association for Competitive Swimming (VACS): June 1978 to April 1989

In the late summer of 1977, I applied for a coaching job with the Tritons of Petersburg but failed to get the job. When it came down to the last two applicants, my resumé was not as extensive as the one who got the job. In April of 1978, the coach who got the job was released by the Tritons. Two of the parents of swimmers on that team called me in Vero Beach to inquire if I would consider taking the position. I returned to Virginia for an interview in May and decided to take the position, because I had started some work in Virginia Swimming which I considered to be important, and the

Tri-Cities team seemed to have greater potential that could help the development of my career at that time. There were only 12 swimmers training that summer but I was told the team had been as many as 75 the previous year and it could be expected it would be again in the fall with new leadership. The 12 who were training that summer seemed to have good potential. In the late summer, I hired Diane Cayce and Mark Kutz to assistant coaching positions in the fall. I worked with Diane for 22 years. Mark did numerous jobs at that point in his life and soon focused on them. Eventually Mark became a very good coach.

In 1978, the Tritons were a YMCA team. The team began a trek upward at YMCA Nationals, which reached 2nd place combined in 1983. At this point, the Triton BOD decided to remove the team from YMCA competition, and changed the name of the team to VACS (the Virginia Association for Competitive Swimming).

This team, with changing members from 1978 through 1989, was life-changing and career-changing. They changed what they had known from a technical sense. They became sophisticated racers. They taught me about training limits, they taught me about human intelligence, they taught me about the mental game, they taught me about GRIT, and they taught me about perspective as it relates to sport. It is impossible to describe the changes those swimmers and families made in my consciousness as it relates to competitive swimming. I was "finding my way" through competition at higher levels, culminating with international competition—and preparation. As swimmers improved through those levels, it was necessary to research and learn. And there was the realization that not all swam for the same reasons, or aspired to compete at higher levels—but each swimmer was equally important to the team in their own ways. I made the decision during these years that I wanted to try to help all swimmers to improve to (at least) the next logical level for the swimmer. And—I wanted swimmers to want that also! This has stayed with me, although the wish comes true in varying degrees at various times, which seem to be somewhat out of my control.

I learned during the years of coaching in the Tri-Cities, that when I tried <u>very</u> hard to be a good coach, swimmers tried <u>very</u> hard to be good swimmers.

There were many great swimmers and many great families with this team. Four of the inaugural class of six, of the Virginia Swimming Hall of Fame were from this team: Whitney Hedgepeth (Olympic Qualifier 1988, Olympic Medalist 1996), Diane Cayce (coached 5 Olympians on 3 different teams), Walter Smith (President of Virginia Swimming, Inc., for many years), and yours truly. One in the next class was from this team and Poseidon Swimming—Rada Owen (2000 Olympic Team Qualifier).

The Tri-cities was a working class metropolitan area. The facilities we used for training were also working class. Some VACS swimmers traveled to a National Championship meet at Mission Viejo, California around 1985. They, and I, were AMAZED by the wonderful facilities of the Mission Viejo Nadadores. We all thought Mission Viejo swimmers would experience culture shock if they were to visit our training facilities. But in the end, water was water!

<u>Poseidon Swimming, Inc.</u>: April 1989 to April 2000

During the 1980's, the two best performing teams in Virginia were VACS of the Tri-Cities and the Briarwood Swim Team in Midlothian, Virginia. The two teams were about 30 miles apart from each other. In 1989, the decision was made by the Board of Directors of each team to merge the two teams, in an effort to build an excellent competitive facility between the two teams, and to benefit from the strength of the two teams together.

Briarwood had a pretty good facility situation but they had experienced 6 head coaches over an 8 year period. VACS did not have great facilities for training, but I had been the head coach for 11 years. The decision was to merge the two teams and that I would be the head coach. This was accomplished in April 1989. The new team was called Poseidon Swimming as an elevation of the Triton name from earlier years.

Unfortunately, a new VACS BOD was elected during that year and they, in a short-sighted decision, chose not to remain in the merger. Diane Cayce and I decided to continue to coach Poseidon along with former Briarwood coaches Joe Bradford and Gwen Braaten.

Without the VACS team in the merger, the overall Poseidon team was reduced as a competitive entity, but the foundation for a great team was still in place. Poseidon Swimming, within a few years, became a force in Virginia Swimming. VACS began to wither in strength as coaching changes happened there.

Poseidon became nationally recognized as swimmers became competitive at every level. Rada Owen qualified for National Championships in high school and for the 2000 Olympic Team during her senior year at Auburn University, and with the leadership of David Marsh. Rada's supporting cast in high school were a wonderful group of girls who set National Age Group records in relays. Boys and girls were scoring at Junior National Championships. The training groups were very strong throughout the program and parental support was amazing. 1996 was a very special year at Poseidon Swimming.

Once again, swimmers were teaching me. Training sessions at Poseidon were extremely competitive. Swimmers were positive while being competitive with each other. This team participated in events outside of practice. Team travel was a norm for senior level swimmers. There were beach trips. There were "get togethers" throughout the year when swimmers would celebrate holidays together. Our senior group had an annual hike at Grandfather Mountain in North Carolina, which was significantly challenging physically and where the weather could be challenging too. They RACED very tough. They were a blast and I loved coaching them.

In 1996, I also started a business, with the Briarwood Aquatics Director, called SwimMetro Management, Inc. The purpose of the business was to manage "summer neighborhood" pools, including hiring, training, and supervising lifeguards. The mission of SwimMetro also included maintenance of property and facilities. I didn't really work at the new business, but I was instrumental in the start-up. Kurt Schuster, my partner, did the work in the field and trained lifeguards. Also, in 1996, I had the idea for a local sports complex modeled after the Olympic Training center ideal. The idea came to me while attending a meeting hosted by the Richmond Sports Backers (Jon Lugbill) at the offices of Richmond Renaissance. The meeting was attended by a group of Richmond sports leaders. Jon asked the question: "What is your greatest need for your programs?" To a person, all answered, "Our greatest need is for better facilities where we can better train our athletes and host high quality events." It occurred to me, if we all needed the same thing, we could do it at one complex on which we could realize economies of scale. I incorporated a non-profit 501c3 company called SportsQuest,Inc. A Board of Directors was formed with representatives from that group of sports team leaders, Jon Lugbill, an accountant, a lawyer, and a sports medicine doctor. I found a landowner (Mark Sowers) who owned 200 acres of land centrally located in Chesterfield County, and he was willing to sell, or lease, land sites to sports organizations at discounted prices. Chesterfield County was invited to place infrastructure on the land in return for the anticipated economic development that would come from the sports teams hosting events. HKS Architects, who designed the Disney Wide World of Sports Complex in Orlando, Florida, designed renderings of the SportsQuest Complex. This business plan had 4 overall objectives:

1. SportsQuest, Inc., would fundraise for all sports using a fundraising professional staff , similar to a collegiate athletic department, and manage the common facilities on the complex.

2. Chesterfield County would build the infrastructure on the complex, allowing Mark Sowers to sell or lease property to sports teams at discounted prices.

3. Mark Sowers would sell or lease property to sports teams, which would build their own facilities, using HKS Architects for design/build.

4. When possible, sports would combine to build facilities that could be shared to reduce costs. For example, facilities such as locker rooms, bathrooms, reception areas, utilities, and electricity could be shared to reduce individual costs to sports teams. The complex would have common areas to be shared as well.

I took a 9-month course in Philanthropy and Fundraising at the University of Richmond, led by Gerald Quigg, the director of fund development following a $50 MM gift from E. Claiborne Robins, which Mr. Quigg multiplied many times.

In 1998, Karen Kelley, who was a member of the Poseidon Board of Directors, proposed that I change my role from head coach to CEO of Poseidon which allowed me to lead SportsQuest while I led Poseidon. The BOD accepted Karen's proposal, and I agreed. Joe Bradford accepted the position of senior coach—and I coached in all groups on a regularly visiting basis.

Tracy Tynan of the Greater Richmond Partnership became interested in the SportsQuest project and helped tremendously in the effort. She was able to gain the assistance of Brailsford & Dunlavey, Inc., which was a leader in the Olympic bid for Washington DC and Baltimore. We were allowed to host meetings at the offices of the Greater Richmond Partnership.

I worked in this way until 2000, when the Poseidon BOD decided to move in another facility direction and presented me with an ultimatum: Stop work on SportsQuest, or stop work with Poseidon.

After a called Board meeting to consider the conundrum, the BOD presented the ultimatum, and I resigned from Poseidon the next day—in April 2000.

This was an unfortunate time for all concerned. The situation was lose-lose as I see it. At the heart of my motivation was to lead Poseidon to a higher level of consciousness, and into a circumstance which would share with multiple sports, as the complex would have been a local training center in "Olympic" sports. I had been to the Olympic Training Center at Colorado Springs many times and had seen athletes transform from their experiences there. I felt, at that time, Poseidon had reached a natural acceptance of accomplishment collectively. A stimulus seemed needed to naturally motivate the club leaders and swimmers to higher performance. SportsQuest was the stimulus—but it failed to stimulate.

I then worked with SwimMetro which was beginning to thrive. I worked there from April 2000 until September 2003. I also coached weekend freestyle workshops for Total Immersion, Inc., from 2000 until 2003. Each of these work situations were excellent experiences and allowed me to develop many wonderful and professional relationships.

<u>QUEST Swimming</u>: September 2003 to the Present

I learned in 2003 that I could (possibly) purchase a pool property from a swim team which owned the property for 1 year. There were changes in that program which made the deal possible. It was purchased by 3 other partners and me. We purchased it by simply taking over the mortgage on the property. Given this method of purchase, there was not a need to put cash down. The 4 partners represented two pool management companies: SwimMetro Management, Inc. ,and Douglas Aquatics, Inc. Eventually, I "bought out" the other partners and gained sole ownership of the property.

The main condition in the original sale was that I would coach the swim team which was based there. It started with about 75 swimmers. It went through a few name changes, but is now QUEST Swimming. I will discuss the business and the related challenges in the following chapter.

QUEST experienced a change in consciousness over the first three years. It started with educating swimmers about technical efficiencies in swimming. The second year was dedicated to using those efficiencies with speed. In the third year, we began to train swimmers to race.

In the second year, I hired John Smithson to assist me. John has experienced every transformation in the team and in the business since then.

The development of QUEST has been different from the other teams with which I worked.

- The swimming demographic is much more competitive. Poseidon still exists and now trains about a mile "down the road." A new 50 Meter facility was built on the other side of the County and they house a swim team that is formed on the business paradigm of lower cost and convenience of practice schedules. They attract a lot of swimmers with the facility and with that business paradigm. There is YMCA swimming in the area. And there is swimming in the Tri-Cities just south of us. And, there is QUEST.

- We are a private enterprise and the other teams are non-profit businesses. Our business goal is to be profitable. Our swimming development goal is to achieve competitive excellence by teaching the art of swimming and perfecting the game of racing.

- Our facilities operate differently. We have two outdoor pools we use for training. One of them is covered by a 20-year-old bubble in the winter and the other pool is an outdoor heated pool. We promote ideal air quality, but we experience some weather elements from being outdoors.

- There is not a Board of Directors, nor an organized volunteer organization that can mandate volunteer hours, nor our business operations. People do volunteer for some of our projects, but it is of their own volition.

- We have an independent fundraising organization but it is not mandatory. All of the funds raised go specifically to families and not to the private enterprise operations.

Swimmers at QUEST have really been special. They have had me at the end of my career which means they have mostly lived the past experiences, the resulting thoughts, and the concepts which are written in this book. They were game to learn and game to race according to the systems put to them by the coaching staff and me.

We have had superb athletes but we continue to coach to move the midline in the center of the bell curve toward excellence. I have been enormously proud of the way QUEST swimmers have performed, but I have been even more proud of how they behave (most of the time). They wear the team uniform with pride. They race tough and respect their fellow competitors. They practice deliberately. We have a saying, "No Brain, No Gain" and I think most of them try to live that saying. They have laughed at my terrible jokes and listened to my terrible singing (without making fun of me…much). We have had swimmers qualify for every Olympic Trials except one. Maddy Banic broke a World Record in 50 Meter Butterfly (SCM). Clark Beach placed 9th in 200 M Backstroke at the last Olympic Trials, and Jeff Newkirk placed 15th in 200 M Freestyle. QUEST is typically in the top 5 at most state championship meets.

The team has grown from 75 swimmers in 2003 to about 275 swimmers in recent years. Swimmers grew through that period of imposed discipline and became self disciplined along the way. They experienced the changes in suits from the full body to the current tech suits. This is a new century and QUEST swimmers taught me about technology, or at least as much as I would learn. The QUEST facility is a "training center." It is used differently from most other pool facilities. We encourage running, playing games freely, climbing trees, and practically any activity that enhances athleticism. Many swimmers like to arrive early to practice so they can play together. Our older swimmers train outdoors year-round. The coldest temperature in which we have practiced is 7 degrees. Training during snow is fun for our swimmers. Coaches are challenged with weather conditions, but the swimmers adapt well in 82 degree water, and the natural air is awesome! My son invented a water aeration system to cool the water during the summer. It works well, keeping water temperatures below 84 degrees during the summer. Altogether, QUEST is different, and we like it that way.

We have a thriving Swim School, which we celebrated with a Grand Opening of a new indoor pool in the spring of 2023.

I retired from coaching in 2019. Chad Onken and John Smithson are now owners and operate the overall business together. They have a five-year plan for facility improvements and further swimmer developments. The QUEST for a bright horizon lives in the people who lead it now.

12 — Buy It and Work It
(Swimmin' Business)

"When someone says they do not have time for something, they have stated a priority, not a fact." Dr. Tom Baerrett: Dare to Dream and Work to Win

The "typical" paradigm for a Club swimming coach in the United States is:

1. A person develops an interest in competitive swimming as a swimmer, or as having some association with a competitive swim team.

2. That person either applies to coach a swim team, or is lured into coaching by some circumstance.

3. Teams are normally controlled by a group of team organizers, or swimmers' parents who form a Board of Directors and a "non-profit" oriented business (501c3) for team operations.

4. Coaches are hired, according to the following factors:

   • Financial capabilities of the team based on numbers of swimmers and fundraising

   • Perceived capabilities of the coach based on experience, education, leadership, etc.

   • Vision, Mission, Values of the team, either perceived or written.

The purpose of this chapter is to differentiate between a private, coach-owned, for profit business paradigm from a Board of Directors controlled, non-profit paradigm as they pertain to: a) control of the team's destiny, b) control of the coache's destiny, c) earnings, and d) personal satisfaction.

Successful club coaches usually trend their teams toward some measures of team improvement whether it be growing the numbers of swimmers on the team, improved team performance on a scoring level or team placement, perceived learning that is taking place which is recognizable from observation, etc.

Club coaches are normally compensated along some scale which is determined by the "non-profit" Board of Directors, as is a coach's ultimate ability to move the team, and his/her career, forward.

Compensation has tended along the scales of school teachers ,as a trend. Head coaches might get comparative compensation to principals in schools; however, club coaches rarely earn similar to professions such as collegiate coaches, medical sales reps, CEOs of companies, or engineers, etc. A club coach's education might be equal to or greater than those of other professions, their leadership might be superior, or their business acumen might be excellent in terms of program growth, team success ,or multi-level benefits to the overall recognition of the team at state, regional, or national levels.

This is not to say that Club coaches should or should not earn more. It is to say that Club coaches are significant in the lives of swimmers for almost a decade of time. They are often very well educated, they are usually great leaders, they influence the flow of dollars, they work different hours of the day, they work away from the deck, and they are considered responsible for the success or failure of the organization as a whole. It seems reasonable that coaches would (at least) be compensated according to the growth in swimmers and revenue which is earned for the organization due to the efforts of coaches.

For example: if a program grows from 100 swimmers to 1000 swimmers at an average of $2,000 per swimmer and the team is able to earn $1,000,000 in fund raising because the team is nationally recognized, that would be $2,800,000 of revenue to the Club. To pay the coach(es) $50,000 to $75,000 or less seems insufficient for what the staff, or the head coach, contributes to those earnings.

I must say at this point that most members of Boards of Directors are well-meaning, good-hearted, interested, and caring people who have the best interests of athletes and the team in mind as they volunteer their time and energy to help to administer swim teams. They tend to give freely of their time and expertise to be part of the solution(s) on many matters at numerous levels of engagement.

However, due to this paradigm of business, a successful coach's life, or the lives of a coaching staff, can and mostly are, limited by the following factors:

- BOD positions are a "political" process; thus, the direction of the team can be subject to change when Board members change.

- Time available and quality of training facilities, based on the amount(s) a BOD is willing to pay for rent.

- The consciousness, or lack of it, by BOD members; that is, (mostly) respective to novice, age group and senior levels of competitive swimming.

- The susceptibility of BOD members to act on rumors and/or "ignorant" perceptions, rather than real-life truth of matters.

There are many other examples, of course. But for the most part, USA Swimming is composed of Clubs that have provided the foundation of competitive swimming, which has led to America being the dominant swimming power in the world. Most of this achievement has been specifically due to Club coaches who coach swimmers over as much as a decade, leading up to their ultimate achievements in the sport.

But – the majority of successful Club coaches in America have stated at one time or another: *"If I had my own pool I could accomplish so much more with my team."*

Honestly, for all of the teams I have coached, I have had the same thought. When I was younger, I felt entirely dependent on others to provide for me as it pertained to my success and my career path. Now, I realize that I was never dependent on others to provide anything for me. I was simply ignorant as to how to provide for myself.

In 2003, I bought a pool.

I needed a lawyer and an accountant, which I had from starting the business of SwimMetro Management, Inc., in 1996. Legal Zoom can also be used for the legal necessities to start a company, and if you have capability with QuickBooks, you can do most of the accounting yourself; however, business accounting is time-consuming, so there is wisdom in hiring an accountant. Having an accountant to update your books quarterly will help when the accountant provides end-of-year tax returns to the IRS. This is a significant time-saver and protects you from fear of audits (mostly).

Sometimes, the coach can interest a lawyer or an accountant to volunteer, to work for their children's fees, or to work for a minimum compensation for the amount of work you need as a small program. The larger and more sophisticated your program becomes though, the more you need to pay for these professionals.

I was 56 years old when I purchased the pool property, but I could have done the same thing when I was 30 years old. I simply assumed a mortgage on an older pool (25 yards, 6 lanes, and a diving well). A neighborhood had aged to the point where there were no longer large groups of young families remaining, and the older families were not motivated to continue caring and paying for the pool upkeep.

Another swim team purchased the pool from the homeowners association but they released their head coach the next year. When I offered to buy the pool and coach the team, they decided it was a win-win, so we made the deal.

That mortgage was the amount of an average house in Midlothian, Virginia, at that time ($225,000). Since I assumed the mortgage, I did not need to pay a down-payment; thus, there was no cash requirement to purchase. I could have done the same thing for much less in the early stages of my career. For comparison, I bought my first home when I was 30 years old (1978) for $49,900 on a 9% VA loan.

QUEST started with 70 competitive swimmers, paying about $2,000 per swimmer per year on average. I was working with about $150,000 per year to run the business. My compensation was almost nil in that first year, but I was the only employee and my work was free. My work ranged from cleaning bathrooms, to vacuuming the pool, to mowing the grounds, to coaching, to administration, and— everything else that needed doing.

I did buy this pool with partners, but I did not need them. I did 100% of the work at this pool, and membership was 100% registered because I was coaching there. The partners were good people but they were part of problems more than part of solutions. Eventually, I bought them out so I could be the only member (owner) of the business.

The business was incorporated as an LLC in 2003, and it remains an LLC even though the previous partners are no longer members. The business is taxed as an S Corporation.

In 2023, it will have been 20 years since I made that purchase. Over the years, I have refinanced the mortgage a couple of times to accommodate some cash flow challenges in the business.

In 2017, the property/business was appraised at $468,000. The property was zoned as residential at that time. It was zoned Residential because it was originally a Homeowners Association property for a community. I rezoned the property when I needed to complete renovations.

In 2020, the property was rezoned to Commercial and

improvements on the pool were made. The deck, the grounds and the clubhouse have been renovated. In 2023, we finished our new pool construction, a $1.7 MM project, to build a teaching pool and a building that will house a reception area, a store, a viewing area, office space, and changing rooms. After the project, the property and business was appraised in 2022 at $2.62 MM.

The QUEST competitive team registered 292 athletes (2021-2022) and our teaching program registered its 500th member in June 2022. Lessons are registered monthly. Revenues for 2022 are anticipated at $1.1 MM and we anticipate that QUEST will generate an additional $1 to $2 MM per year within 3 years of the construction of the teaching pool.

AND—QUEST is altogether in control of its destiny. The Vision, Mission, and Values which support the Philosophy of its programming is unchanging (except for positive change). The facilities are ever improving and cannot be lost to us by other people who are not primarily concerned with QUEST success; that is, we are not renting from other pool owners who have other priorities for themselves.

This all sounds positive and good. It is very good in the overall scheme of things. But, I must say, it has not been easy. Also, I prefer this paradigm for myself because I was (mostly) responsible for the positives and the negatives along the way. I was not limited except by my own motivation and capabilities to continue.

The negatives should be described for those who may not be inclined toward this paradigm:

1. There have been (many) times when I have been more tired from work than I have been before in my life.

2. There have been times when there has not been enough money to pay business expenses on time, and in full. I had to find a way, even when I did not know how.

3. Team members/parents vote with their dollars; therefore, one wonders when there is disagreement or lack of good performance what they will do. This causes some nervousness, or questioning oneself at times.

4. As the business grows and becomes more complicated, more people are dependent on the success of the business, and you. QUEST has about 25 employees now.

5. Available time, to be with family members and friends or to have a social life, is on a sliding scale which is not according to the wishes of those people, nor oneself. These factors are according to what the business and the work allows. This is also something that club coaches experience, whether hired by an organization, or whether you own your business.

I did reach a physical point of diminishing returns (personally) between the ages of 65 and 70. I had a "minor" stroke in 2015 and back surgery in 2017. I was able to recover well though, and there are no side effects now.

I have been retired from coaching since January of 2019. My health is VERY good now; therefore, I know it was the work of the business which was affecting my health negatively- at my age.

For those coaches who are so inclined, I wish I had known what I know now when I was 30 years of age. How many times have you heard or said the same thing? This is one reason for this book. I am hopeful that some younger Club coaches can benefit from my experience, specifically as a Club coach.

I could have and would have controlled my own destiny through private ownership. While the work has been difficult at times, this work has been different for me; that is, I don't seem to mind doing any kind of work or task when I tell myself to do it. However, I tend to weigh the work and the compensation when someone else is telling me to do it.

I also love the notion that my team can be as good as I can imagine without a second opinion which might alter the direction in ways other than those which seem right to me. This is not to say that I need to dictate the direction of the Team without feedback, but it is to say that I prefer making my own mistakes and correcting them. I do not like others to make mistakes for my team where I can be held accountable or voted out of relevant decision-making. I consider myself to be professional at what I do. I consider board members to be volunteers who control my profession.

Had I started the business in my early career years rather than at 56 years old, my health from 65 to 70 would have been better (I think). I am sure that the most challenging years would have been when I was young enough to handle the physical demands of the work more easily. The question then would have been whether I was mature enough to handle the emotional challenges. I think so, because there were significant emotional challenges anyway and I made it, despite the emotional immaturity of my early 30's as I recall them.

In 2018, I participated on a panel which discussed the idea of owning your program and your pool versus owning your program without owning your pool. All of the other panel members stated they preferred owning their programs but not their pools. The others shared that they knew the work needed to keep pools operating and they did not want to do it.

But for me, I don't consider that one owns their program if they cannot control their pool time and training circumstances.

A good example was the use of pool time and space during the COVID-19 fears, which caused shut downs for most facilities. We did close our operations for a short time as President Trump called for in March of 2020. But we reopened on our own terms on June 1st and continued operations for all levels of programming, whereas many of our competitors in the market ceased operations altogether, or limited their operations in large part. The coaching staff was

<u>instrumental in this</u>. They coached 1 swimmer per lane each hour of the day at our 2 pools from early in the morning until late evening, from June until August. They concentrated on technical perfection during these months. They also scheduled zoom presentations of recognized USA athletes—and dry land sessions.

Almost all small business owners are confronted with similar challenges to their time and compensation.

As I mentioned earlier in this book, I consider the flow of money to be much like the flow of a river upon which one lives. It is most important to be aware of your dependence on the good flow of the river (cash flow) to provide for your needs. As long as the river flows well, you can take from it, and provide well for you and your loved ones. If the river's flow is obstructed or depleted, especially when it is for some reason that you caused, it will also limit the ability for the river (cash flow) to provide.

Cash and money are the same. It has to flow in business. The business owner needs to be aware of it constantly. It will not always flow sufficiently according to your wishes or your needs, but you have to be aware so you can put it back to good flow when there is an obstruction. You <u>have to</u> find a way.

There is not a day when I fail to look at the business bank account to study cash flow.

One lifestyle characteristic that has been useful to me as a business owner is that I don't spend freely on personal wants. My wardrobe is singular, my vehicle is utilitarian (a pickup truck that lasts), I take affordable vacations when I take them, etc.

For example, between marriages, I rented an upstairs apartment of a two story house, and I had no furniture, nor heat for almost 2 years. I was altogether content and happy to live that way.

Therefore, I have been able to save money well. This tendency in my nature has enabled me to loan money to the business in time(s) of need.

Altogether, operating your business is similar to the lessons you share with competitive swimmers:

- Begin with the end in mind.

- Take appropriate actions in the moment that lead to success.

- Be aware and cognizant at ALL times.

- Be consistent daily with good habits and deliberate practice.

- Be positive.

- Never "give up."

- Believe in yourself.

- Have "GRIT."

Marketing matters in this business paradigm. It is important to differentiate the advantages of your program versus others. Specifically, it is (to be able) to articulate a positive difference between what is done at your program and the others in your market. This does not necessarily mean that one is better than others and should not be stated in those terms. That is for the people in the market to determine for themselves.

At QUEST, we summarize what we do in our motto: *We are dedicated to teaching the Art of Swimming and to perfecting the Game of Racing.*

We have a way of teaching and training at QUEST. It is somewhat unique in certain ways. But more importantly, all staff members are dedicated to being consistent throughout all levels of the program. It is observable; that is, there is a difference in the look of most QUEST swimmers when they move through the water. It is a recognizable difference for many observers. Methods in meet warm-ups are noticeably different. This is not according to me. It is from objective feedback of others over the years.

WE market this in as many ways as we can.

Generally, swim teams don't market, but we have found it to be important to our business.

A good example of this concept is that during the beginning of the COVID-19 pandemic, we marketed swimming pools as one of the safest places to exercise since, when swimming, every body cell and opening was open to chlorinated water, which kills viruses.

Henry Ford once said: "A man who stops advertising to save money is like a man who stops a clock to save time." I agree. As a private business owner, there is wisdom in marketing to attract families into your programs.

This chapter was a driving motivation to write this book. It is to show that there is an answer to that statement made by practically all successful USAS Club coaches at one time or another: "*If I could only have my own pool, I could actually accomplish the potential of this team of athletes—and myself—better.*"

Places and circumstances differ. What was done and is continuing to be done at QUEST is not the only way to find an answer to the statement. But the basics are about the same.

"Own your pool. Own your water. Own your program." Then you can use the qualities and the skills you use to coach people to be successful in swimming to be successful in your business – and – to achieve your expectations as a USAS Club coach.

I will say, from a personal perspective, the time that I have owned my business as a swim coach, has been the most pleasurable and rewarding because I have not felt the need to adhere to the whims and natures of people who could change my direction for the team indiscriminately. QUEST does not have the best pool facility, or even close to it, but I do think we make the best use of what we have—and we are (usually) competitive.

QUEST continues to place in the top five teams in all levels of Virginia Championships, and to qualify swimmers to National level competitions. This is not to my ultimate satisfaction really. But swimmers in Chesterfield County are split among four teams, which split swimmers in the County in four directions for participation. Each team has a differing philosophy, administration, and methods for athlete development. If the four teams, (Poseidon, QUEST, SwimRVA, and NOVA-South) could work together, much more could be accomplished on many levels. NOVA, of Virginia, serves Henrico County which is north of the James River (virtually as one organization) and it has achieved greater results – as a result.

It's interesting—for all of my career leading up to QUEST, I always had some accessibility to 50-Meter pools for my teams. Since QUEST, this has not been the case. There have been none. I always thought it was to my advantage to have a long course pool for training swimmers – but, since I have not had a long course pool for training, I have never considered it to my dis-advantage not to have it. I found other ways to compensate and they have been successful.

Ways that we used to compensate were and are:

- Distance greater than the expected race distance to equal the expected time and stroke counts for races.

- Resistance in the water.

- Vertical kicking.

- During Peak Performance especially, times for 225 yards is (practically) the same as times for 200 meters in long course.

This fact is used extensively.

There are other programs that have been successful in ownership: SwimAtlanta built a network of pools for training, and combined competitive swimming with pool management for successful business; NITRO in Texas has been successful with private ownership to operate competitive swimming with swim lessons in their own pool(s).

USAS has information on their web site concerning private ownership that can be very helpful, although it might lend to the idea that it is complicated to accomplish. As I have shared in this book, a lawyer and an accountant can get you going to incorporate, and to handle taxes, respectively. Otherwise, one needs excellent leadership skills, excellent coaching skills to attract swimmers, and commitment to do whatever it takes to be competitive in the business market, as well as the market of competitive sport.

It is a good idea to know your competition and to have confidence that you can compete; that is, to have a decent location, to know what will be your price points, and to have a system of coaching that will attract a team of swimmers, and/or lessons that you offer.

I know this seems to be over-simplified, but complication may cause you to have reservations. It is fairly simple. Money into the business needs to be equal to money out of the business in order to break even. Add a percentage, and to that extent, the business can be profitable and the owner has compensation. Simple. Not easy necessarily, but simple. As I stated earlier, legal counsel and an accountant are helpful.

Government regulations and taxes can be hurdles to leap, but you tend to learn them in the first year and adjust fees accordingly.

QUEST Boosters: There is a fundraising organization that helps swimmers and swimmers' families at QUEST. They are 501c3 and they can also help others in the swimming world. All of the money they raise is used to the benefit of swimmers and their families. None of the money they raise is used in the operations of QUEST Swimming: that is the LLC.

However, QUEST Boosters have paid for awards, banquets and ceremonies, training equipment like buckets, apparel, travel funds for National level athletes attending National competitions, social events, etc.

The difference between QUEST Boosters and other 501c3 organizations which operate swim teams is that others use money raised to pay for operations such as compensation for coaches, pool rental, etc. The BODs of those organizations also control all decision making for the teams for which they are formed.

The BOD of QUEST Boosters has no such control of any decision-making regarding QUEST Swimming—the LLC, the Team nor the Lessons, nor the property. The relationship is when families participate in their fundraising, they know that 100% of the money raised will be used directly for swimmers but it is still helpful to QUEST Swimming—the LLC—because services QUEST Boosters families would otherwise be paid with surcharges, assessments or fees, or they would not exist.

It is my wish that some coaches will benefit from the information in this book (altogether) to help USAS Club coaches. I also hope some coaches will gain an answer to the statement so many of us make: *"if I had my own pool I could do this so much better."*

13 — PARENTS: in a Triangle

When we structure our support groups, we do it in the form of a triangle where the swimmer is placed at the top of a triangle, the coach is in one lower corner, and parents are placed at the other corner of the triangle. This is truly how it should work. Parents and coaches should support the swimmer.

The parental role is to provide swimmers with their opportunities, their comfort, their nutrition, their transportation, their apparel and equipment, their financial needs, and positive emotional support.

The coach's role is to provide the information, the training, the competitive experience, and a safe environment for improving their capabilities as a competitive swimming athlete.

If the roles of the parent and the coach overlap each other, there is usually confusion for the athlete which usually causes some detriment to performance eventually.

But there is something to know and realize about parents. That is, parents can be "blinded by their love for their children." I learned this when my own son was 4 years old.

It happened one day in 1976. I lived in an upstairs corner apartment with a balcony in Norfolk, Virginia. I watched from the balcony as my son and a neighbor's son played at a playground adjacent to my apartment. At one point, both wanted to swing on the swing at the same time. There was only one swing. The boys began to argue about this and the neighbor's son, who was 6-years-old, pushed my son, who was 4-years-old, out of the way so he could swing and my son fell from the push.

The next thing I remember is waving my index finger at the 6-year-old and starting to speak to him harshly. I realized what I was doing mid-sentence, my pointing finger waving back and forth. And I collected myself.

I then changed my tone, suggesting quietly that both boys could swing, but they would need to take turns since there was only one swing. As I returned to my viewing spot, I realized that I did not remember going back through my apartment, down the stairs and over to the swing set.

I was blinded by my love for my son. Interestingly, the 6-year-old let Ryan swing first. He was explaining to Ryan how to swing since it was Ryan's first time on it. Ryan barely moved on the swing.

Then I began to think about the parents of swimmers I coached. I realized that I was blinded by the love for my son and acted out of pure emotion. This insight gave me much more patience in emotional circumstances with parents who seemed to behave poorly – most of the time. Patience was not a natural virtue for me when I was young, but I do think I practiced patience in a better way as I matured.

Parents like to give their children pointers to help them perform better; however, it can be both a problem and a solution for the swimmer.

My son taught me another pretty good lesson when he was 13. He had moved into my training group for the first time since he started swimming at 8 years old. So I was now driving him to practice and home from practice. For a couple of weeks, I talked to him about the practice when we drove home.

After about 2 weeks, I noticed Ryan was gazing out of the window and seemingly paying no attention to my words. So I asked him, "Ryan, I am talking to you – are you listening?" He said, "No Dad." I said, "Why not? I'm trying to help you." He said, "Dad, we were just at the pool for two hours and you were my coach. Now we are driving home and you are my Dad. If you want to tell me about swimming, tell me when you are my coach. Don't tell me when you are my Dad." He drew the line for me quickly as it pertained to what was appropriate.

Parents should support their children—and try to resist the tendency to give coaching tips that are better left to the coaching staff.

Parents can help children by realizing themselves, and helping their children to learn, that there is high value in doing "hard things" and/or things that seem inconvenient. This is particularly the case for teenage children. There are several inconveniences which are normal for year-round Club swimming. The time of day for practices, being wet and dry, breathing in indoor pools, temperatures in outdoor pools, swim meets on weekends, etc., are some of the inconveniences.

For teens especially, there are hard choices to make. Social life is affected; a disciplined scheduling of time is necessary; becoming self-reliant in new ways is mandated; and many other circumstances make life increasingly complicated as swimmers grow year to year. Practice gets more demanding, physically and mentally. Individual behavior in "stressful" group settings needs to be learned which often reduces self-importance for the benefit of the larger group or the team.

These are all hard things for teens and for the Club coach. Often, it is the case that people at adolescent ages will want to lessen their commitment, or quit altogether, when things seem too hard for them to handle. These are times when parents and coaches need to provide education on the high value of doing hard things. In a word, GRIT has been popularized to describe one who stays on course through hard or inconvenient times to ultimate success (or failure) because there is learning either way, which will be the characteristic which enables one to navigate through life's inevitable challenges. Over the years, I have heard many more times from swimmers who share, as adults, that they were glad they finished [than were glad they quit.] I have also heard from many, who regret at the wonderment of what they might have accomplished had they continued in the sport – but unfortunately, they will never know.

This occurrence seems to happen more in recent decades than it did when I was in my 30's and 40's and even my 50's. It seems the result of a combination of kids having less exposure to hard things during growth and development and parents not willing to require them to press through hard times to complete a commitment. This is not altogether the truth of the matter, but it seems more prevalent since about 2000 than before 2000.

It is hard to require. It is easier to say, "It is their decision" and let them quit. Emotions around these decisions are normal. But to the extent that the decision can be made intellectually, it will be a better decision.

Parents are part of solutions to all situations that involve their children from a support standpoint. They do 10,000 things that are needed to raise their children to be healthy, educated, and spiritually right.

And – their children belong to them, not to the coach. It is the coach's responsibility to educate parents on the role of a good parent in supporting the swimmer; however, the coach should not expect that it will always be as you might imagine it should be.

During teen years, the luck of the draw is the case. I have seen, what I consider to be good parents have children who did some bad things during teen years, and I have seen what I consider to be bad parents have good kids during teen years. The truth of it is that the values of parents which are evident in childhood will return to young adults, regardless of teen behaviors for the most part.

Parents mostly get limited opportunities to raise teenagers, so they are learning as they go. No two children are the same, even when they are siblings. Just because a family has had one child go through teen years, it does not mean that the next child will be the same. Almost all parents are trying their best to be the best parents they can be.

Most people are good. I have observed very few people involved in swimming who I would judge to be bad people. There can be some bad decisions, and people can behave in embarrassing ways, but that doesn't make them bad people. This is also true for coaches.

In other words, I have not known people who would rob a bank, or hurt others violently, etc. There are certainly people who behave poorly, show their tempers, and feel emotions of all kinds relating to their children, especially if they feel their child is being treated unfairly.

The coach needs to be the "adult" in relationships with parents, regardless of age differences, if parents are acting immaturely about their children.

It is important on all levels to modify behavior when needed to keep people within the guidelines of good actions. This can sometimes cause the coach to be forceful, but there is a difference between being forceful to keep behavior within normal boundaries and having judgment that a person is inherently bad.

To think of them as bad is to put an impasse between good people. This is counter-productive.

This thought process as it relates to swimmers' parents is after 50 years of coaching. I have had my share of confrontations with parents. I would say now that none ever ended well if I became emotional about the situations or circumstances.

Every parent knows that time with their child is limited to those years before they leave home, which is also the time when they will leave you as their Club swim coach.

Every moment is precious. Let's all enjoy them.

14 — Alone Together
"Smellin' the Barn"

Time as defined is: the system of those sequential relations that any event has to any other, as past, present, or future; indefinite and continuous duration regarded as that in which events succeed one another. Dictionary.com

This seems to me a good definition of time, since I am retired from coaching, but not from owning the business.

I retired from coaching right around my 71st birthday. Just like athletes need to listen, and be aware of their bodies, I needed to listen to mine at that time. I still enjoyed coaching, and I felt I was contributing to helping swimmers realize their quests for success, but I was physically drained. It was also now or never that I could (and should) pay attention to my loved ones as they wished from me.

I continue to work in the business, given the construction project (of the teaching pool). The new pool is now complete and the Grand Opening was celebrated on February 27, 2023.

But I sold my home in Midlothian, Virginia, and made the move with my wife, Jeannie, back to Vero Beach, Florida. We built a new home which is several hundred yards from the Indian River and about 1 mile from the Atlantic Ocean—"as the crow flies." We actually ride a couple of miles, cross a bridge over the Indian River, and we are at the beach. We have a puppy named Vero as of May 2, 2022. I'm not sure why we did this this late in life, but it is done.

I speak with my son weekly and get the news on his wonderful family: his wife Carrie, and the four grandchildren (Cody, Jayce, Leah, and Rylan). I also stay aware of the business of SwimMetro since I gifted my shares of that company to Ryan. We like to talk about his work and the business of SwimMetro.

We are many hours closer to our daughter Julie, who lives in Rincon, Puerto Rico, and operates a business of 30 riding horses. Julie takes people on beach and trail rides in the mornings and the evenings. She is hard working with that many horses to keep healthy and working. She enjoys surfing when waves are up. They are always up during "winter" months there. Rincon is called the Hawaii of the East and surfers go there in big numbers during that time.

I have negotiated an eventual installment sale of the business to Chad Onken and John Smithson. Chad, a former swimmer with the Poseidon team, is an accomplished coach in his own right. He is highly motivated to be the business owner.

John Smithson, at this time has my mind plus his own with which to work. He, while working side by side all of the years since 2004, learned everything I could share, and experienced every up and down of the business for almost 20 years. He is an excellent coach. He understands the nature of this business intuitively and intellectually.

Chad leads the Swim School for QUEST, and John leads the competitive swim team as primary responsibilities. Both have responsibilities in the others' primary areas because the business is the sum of the parts to equal the whole.

Both oversee and lead the business of QUEST. Both are responsible for the future of QUEST as it relates to the Vision, Mission, Values—and business strategies. They are forward looking, equal to the present and understand what has happened in the past. They are already much better than me.

The installment payments of the sale will help us to maintain our (Jeannie, Vero, and me) current level of life through the end of it, at least as I have it planned. I have not gained wealth from the business, but I am proudly part of the productive middle class in America.

Being a USAS Club coach has life challenges which are

unavoidable. It starts with the working hours which are outside of normal times in a working day. They are before and after school hours. They are weekends and holidays.

The hours put strains on family life, especially, and social life, that are unsettling at times to say the least. There is an ongoing tension between the perceived importance of work and the importance of loved ones, or life as most people perceive it.

The illusion for those with whom you live, more often than not, seems like the work takes a place in your consciousness that is most important. For coaches, we know in our hearts and minds this is not the case. Spouses and children are uppermost in our consciousness, in terms of importance, but we have so little control over elements of the work such as facilities, utilization of facilities, working hours, meet specifications, clientele, etc., that other facets of life fall into the open spaces.

If you add business and facility maintenance to the responsibilities, you have a VERY full-time job.

In the end, after all of the trials and tribulations in one's relationships, it seems like there comes perspective for all concerned, and life returns to "normal," but much of the time along the way is spent in constant justification for "the work" and explaining the importance of people in your life.

Life is like the river too. It flows and brings one in contact with people for whom you care deeply (and not), circumstances to your advantage (and not), colleagues with whom you have joyful competition (and not), and so the river of life flows on.

I believe all of us would take do-overs if we could correct mistakes we made and not make other mistakes. I certainly feel that way at this stage of my life.

But that being stated, I hope I have been good to people by and large. I hope that nothing I did caused irreparable harm to any person. To anyone for whom that might not be the case, I sincerely apologize to them. For all that I question inwardly, I have confessed and asked forgiveness from Jesus, who gives ultimate forgiveness for life's mistakes.

I have (mostly) done what I thought needed to be done to be successful at my craft, regardless of how much time it took, when and where it needed to be done, or how difficult it seemed. I started in this way as a very young, single person. I never felt myself to be a very talented person on any level, but I did think I was extremely dedicated in my will to succeed; that is, to do "whatever it takes." I never changed from this basic premise, even when my life changed with marriage, family, successful moments, or disappointments.

Whether successful or not, I think I did well at leaving the past in the past regardless of disappointments ,and starting anew with focus on the present and the future.

From past to present, there have been people who were critical to the growth of teams, esprit de corps, technical advances, race performances, and team scores. It is not possible to truly describe their contributions in this chapter. I could probably write a book on each one of them. Coaches are mentioned here but there were parent volunteers, other family members, and people in the overall communities who were special and valuable to the various programs.

1. *Bounty Otters Swim Club* at Old Dominion University - Beth Holmquist was an amazing coach, but she was also a key assistant in the overall organization. She was empathetic, motivating, technical, and part of every solution. Others at BOSC were great motivators and willing to do anything needed to improve swimmers. Their energy and focus on our challenges was excellent. In 1976, we had too little pool time for the number of swimmers and the various skill levels

we coached. All of us became masters at pool utilization in a short time, and BOSC managed to win the Virginia Age Group Championships that year.

2. *Tritons/VACS* – Diane Cayce, Mark Kutz, Terry Laughlin, Geoff Brown, and Jan Pingle –

> Diane Cayce was a constant stabilizing force and a tremendous coach for the age group swimmers here and at Poseidon. She was very creative and used planned strategies to move swimmers toward senior level preparation. Mark Kutz worked for a short time but was most helpful in the start-up of the program.
>
> Terry Laughlin worked for one year but was an equal in development of senior level swimmers. We shared many thoughts and ideas before, during the year, and afterward which I consider of immense value to my coaching. RIP.
>
> Geoff Brown merged a group of swimmers from the west end of Richmond with VACS for two years. Geoff was, and is, an excellent swimming coach with a high IQ for teaching and training swimmers. We had many extensive and enjoyable conversations during this time.
>
> Jan Pingle, a great parent for Thad and Anna Pingle, was an extremely focused coach for age group swimmers and a wise presence on the team.

3. *Poseidon Swimming, Inc.* – Joe Bradford, Gwen Braaten, Diane Cayce, Ted Sallade –

> Joe Bradford was head coach for the Briarwood team in the merger of VACS and Briarwood, and assisted me with the senior level of the Poseidon team. He was a very good swimmer for Briarwood before and intensely loyal to the team. He was an excellent worker with many additional skills which were helpful to Poseidon.

Gwen Braaten – Gwen had worked for Briarwood, and also swam at Briarwood. She coached novice swimmers and made the experience great fun for them. She was a dedicated teacher and coach.

Diane Cayce – continued to serve Poseidon as she had done with Tritons/VACS. Her swimmers loved her practice planning, her goal setting, and her personality. They were completely confident at race time.

Ted Sallade – joined the staff after the merger, but made transitions from an excellent age group coach to an excellent senior coach.

4. *QUEST* – John Smithson, Chad Onken, Amy Howard, Chrissie (Hite) Callis, Carrie Jones,Chris Bushelman, Kelly Cleary, Anastasia Carneal, Joanie Elmore.

John Smithson – John started working at QUEST in 2004 at 26 years old (I think). He was first a student of the QUEST way. He is completely loyal to it. He has depth of understanding, he has added his own thoughts to it, and he is now the leader of it. He has done the same with the business. He is in a word – QUEST.

Chad Onken – Chad swam at Poseidon from 13 to 18 years of age. He's kept in touch from his high school graduation and returned to enable my retirement. He has been a leader as a coach, a business entrepreneur, the Swim School administrator, and as co-owner of QUEST. His value in those elements has been indescribable. All is better since Chad moved his family to Midlothian and engaged with QUEST Swimming, the Swim School, and the business altogether.

Amy Howard – The best thing I can say about Amy is that she has coached and led our age group program with all of the skill, enthusiasm, and dedication of Diane Cayce. As a General's daughter and a former major in the US Army, a William and Mary swimmer and graduate, she has leadership that runs through her nervous system. QUEST was lucky when she developed an interest in our way and decided to help the program.

Chrissie (Hite) Callis – Chrissie was another Poseidon swimmer who developed an interest in coaching and found her way to QUEST. She also has a daughter, Emerson, who is now competing at a very high level, much like Chrissie did before. Chrissie leads our novice program with patience, creativity, and a dedication to our way of teaching and training. She understands the long game intuitively; that is, she teaches good fundamentals with the knowledge that her work will turn into racing skills in later development and training.

Carrie Jones – Carrie came to QUEST through masters swimming and local coaching. She also married the brother of one of our early great swimmers named Kaitlin Jones. Carrie and Chrissie work with QUEST novice swimmers as an excellent team.

Chris Bushelman – worked with Chad (Onken) at YOTA (YMCA of the Triangle Area) in North Carolina. He found his way to QUEST after Chad was hired at QUEST. Chris has experience in team development and coaching athletes through National levels. Chris is a student of the QUEST Way, and are eagerly contributing to swimmers at QUEST.

Kelly Cleary – Kelly was first a master's swimmer at QUEST, coached novice swimmers, and eventually set our Swim School into motion. She is an enthusiastic teacher and leader in that programming.

Anastasia Carneal – Anastasia, a fellow Newport News, Virginia, native, became a leader in the SwimMetro lifeguard system, started teaching swim lessons at QUEST, and became a leader in the Swim School. Her wonderful personality, her natural leadership capabilities, and her teaching skills have guided her toward important leadership responsibilities in the QUEST Swim School.

Joanie Elmore – Joanie is relatively new to teaching in the QUEST swim school. However, she is a former swimmer for BOSC at Old Dominion University and she is an excellent teacher who is also a leader for the Swim School. There was "something about her" as a young swimming athlete which remains to this day. She is approachable, trustworthy, and attractive for swimmers and families. She is a new asset to the Swim School.

There have also been volunteers throughout my career who have always been part of solutions. There are too many to name but I am eternally grateful to ALL of them. USAS Club coaching is impossible without them.

The people who have passed through my life have been amazing! Athletes, athletes' families, volunteers, staff members, colleagues, and my family have made my coaching life and my business life a journey of immense personal reward. They have been – AMAZING too!

On another subject, I always thought I should coach the team that hired me, or later when I hired myself, so I chose not to apply to be a National team coach. I was very interested in the National team and USA success, but I never thought my coaching would make much difference for those athletes; whereas, I thought I was making a significant difference day to day for the athletes I coached on my home team.

When life has been complicated, I have tried to keep it simple in terms of my work. I have been able to compartmentalize my consciousness, which has been most helpful when I owned my business.

In May 2022, I was inducted into the swimRVA Hall of Inspiration. Ironically, it is ALL of the people with whom I have been fortunate to have in my life who have inspired me.

Thanks to ALL of YOU for EVERYTHING!

— Appendix A — QUEST Handbook

Organization of the Sport

Governing Bodies:

- <u>FINA</u>: International federation of all national governing bodies.

- <u>USA Swimming, Inc.</u>: National governing body of US Swimming. Headquartered at the US Olympic Training Center – Colorado Springs, CO

- <u>Virginia Swimming, Inc.</u>: One of the Local Swim Committees (LSC) that implements USA Swimming rules and regulations at the local level [typically located within state boundaries].

QUEST MISSION, VISION, AND VALUES

Mission:
The Mission of Quest is stated in its motto: "We are dedicated to teaching the Art of Swimming and to perfecting The Game of Swimming."

Vision:
The Vision of Quest is to be the finest competitive swimming experience possible – from novice to nationals (and beyond) – for all of Greater Richmond.

Values:
Competitive Excellence:

Competitive
com; together + petere; to desire – coming together to elevate the possibilities for achieving desired performance results.

*To Compete is to strive with others, not against others!

Excellence
ex; out of + cellere; to rise – outstandingly good of its kind.

Competitive Excellence is the purpose of our team; that is, to strive with competitors to enable our team members to rise out of their current abilities and into new realms of possibilities.

Goal Setting:
"Seek and ye shall find." Dreams are wiser than men.

Team:
"One finger can't lift a pebble."

Gradualness:
Each level of learning is a foundation for the next level. The stronger the foundation, the better the chances for the next success.

Balance:
"Search the outer limits for greatness, but return to the norm for rest - before the next great event"

Commitment:
"If your mind isn't clouded by unnecessary things, this is the best season of your life." – Wu-Men

Sportsmanship:
"Play fair, lose without complaint and win without gloating"

QUEST PHILOSOPHY

QUEST goals are also defined in its Motto: "*Quest is dedicated to teaching The Art of Swimming and to perfecting The Game of Racing.*"

"It is good to have an end to journey toward, but it is the journey that matters in the end." – Ursula K LeGuin

The first step to great performance is the mastery of proper fundamentals. It is said that one must repeat perfection 10,000 times to master a skill; therefore, when a mistake is made, the process begins again. Fundamentals of aquatic movement are simple but not easy. Fundamentally, one must:

1. Breathe rhythmically and timely: Achieve a perfectly horizontal line for least resistance. Maintain the longest line possible for an optimal time. Generate power from the core body; that is, synchronize movement that moves from the core and ends in the extremities.

2. Challenges arise in the fact that "feel for the water" is not constant and that bodies are ever-changing.

3. Altogether, there must be an everlasting commitment to proper fundamentals of movement in water. This effort will maximize potential power and speed. It will also diminish the potential for injuries that can occur during training.

4. But - the Game of Racing is what we love! Take it out FAST? Build to WIN? THE RACE is the FUN from the beginning of the sport. At QUEST, we want to keep the racing spirit on and on.

Goal Setting gives purpose to practice. Goals are not so much to be the focus of competition. Goals provide enthusiasm during easier stages of the process and commitment during more challenging times. For younger swimmers, this may simply be to win races. For the most seasoned swimmers, goals tend to be multi-dimensional.

For example, they might be specific to:
Advancement to a new level
Handling pressure in highly competitive circumstances
A performance time
Achieving the perfect race
Winning a race with specific competitor(s)

Steps to increase numbers of repetitions at elevated speeds require a gradual adaptation. Likewise, introduction of additional dry land exercise and/or water resistance is factored into seasonal planning. This concept of "gradualness" is central to the philosophy of improvement within QUEST. It will apply in practice and in racing strategy.

The "theory of readiness" also applies. Given equal applications to practice(s), some are ready before others and will realize the benefits of their efforts accordingly. This is as it is in learning to walk as the first significant physical skill in childhood. Some walk before others. The first walkers are not necessarily the best walkers for all time; likewise, in swimming, it is not the case that the first to achieve a competence is necessarily the best into the future. Patience is the virtue that allows potential development over time.

Another underlying theme to the QUEST experience is the development of "the athlete." It is considered that a better athlete can be a better swimmer; therefore, we concentrate on total athletic qualities such as:

Balancing the elements of training for sport and for "life" outside of sport is a constant challenge for all individuals, family, friends, and coaches. This is understood from the beginning.

Philosophically, QUEST claims that balance is critical to longevity in any endeavor. BUT – there is also an acknowledgement that one might require extremes to elevate consciousness to the highest levels. Our method is to thoroughly communicate to all with a [need to know] when challenges will press some outer limits, and when a return to "normalcy" will occur.

We hope that swimmers who begin in the QUEST competitive program will realize a "totally" valuable experience from their years in the program. A journey of a thousand miles begins with one breath.

Learn the Art of Swimming and play the Game of Racing.

"For the raindrop, joy is entering the river." – Ghalib

PARENTS' ROLE IN QUEST PROGRAM

The Triangular Relationship

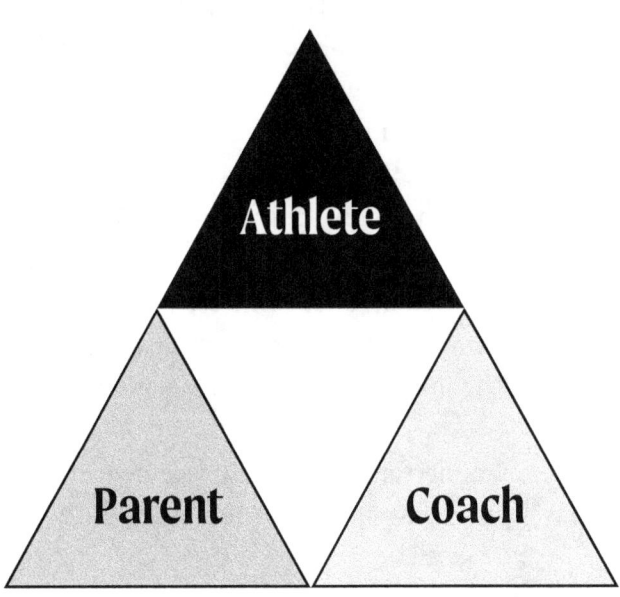

The triangle is symbolic. The swimmer is at the peak of the triangle because he/she is attempting to meet his/her highest potential. The parents and coaches are at the base positions because they represent the support needed for the swimmer to reach the peak levels of their potential. For the swimmer to have a steady experience in the sport, the lines between each of the points need to hold as true and as straight as possible.

With QUEST, each partner in the relationship has a defined role. The role of the parents is an extension of the parental role in the home. Parents should provide the necessities of competitive swimming: uniform, caps, goggles, towels, etc., and whatever time can be spared to insure a quality existence for the program. The swimmer should feel safe and supported in his/her relationship with the parent.

Coaches are also teachers. Their role is to teach fundamental techniques and racing strategies. They offer feedback and judgment on performances. Coaches encourage the risk taking needed for higher levels of consciousness. They are responsible for the philosophical administration of the club, the details of practice and meet performance. It is important for parents and coaches to realize that they share parts of one role, which is to support the swimmer's pursuit of personal excellence. In final decision making, the coaches must understand that parents have ultimate power and rights concerning home matters and related choices. Parents must understand that coaches have final responsibility for team matters such as practice schedules, group placements, meet schedules, event choices, relay selections, attendance policies, and discipline. The swimmer's role is to maximize his/her efforts in the pursuit of peak performance and to be involved productively within the team setting.

Communication, understanding, and involvement are the elements of success within the triangle relationship, just as within any relationship.

Parents' Guidelines

You have done wonders to raise your child. You create the environment in which he/she is "growing up." Your child is a product of your values, the structure you have provided, and the model you have been for them. Human nature, however, is such that people can lose some of their ability to remain detached in matters concerning their child(ren). The following guidelines will help you keep your child's development in the proper perspective.

Every individual learns at a different rate and responds differently to various methods of presentation. Allow time for mastery.

It takes a great deal of the swimmer's attention to master the skills of proper stroke technique. Ninety-eight percent of humans are unnatural in water. Water excellence can be learned, but at varying rates. It is important to remain focused on basic skills until they are learned because these new sets of habits are the basis for later improvement.

Plateaus can occur at one time or another in every swimmer's experience. Plateaus can be in competition and in training. A plateau signifies the swimmer has mastered lower order skills, but he/she is not sufficiently automatic to leave the attention free to attack newer, higher-order skills.

Swimmers under 10 years old are often inconsistent. This can be frustrating for the parent, coach, and swimmer alike! We must be patient in order to permit these youngsters to learn to love the sport.

It is the coach's job to offer constructive criticism of a swimmer's performance. It is a parent's job to supply the unconditional love, recognition, and encouragement necessary to help the young athlete feel good about himself.

If you have questions about your child's training or team policies, contact the coach. Criticizing the coach in front of swimmers undermines the coach's authority and breaks the swimmer-coach support necessary for maximum success. It is for this reason that we ask parents not to actively participate in coaching in any manner.

Be sure that your child swims because he/she wants to. People may resist things that they "have to do." Self motivation is the stimulus of all successful swimmers who go the distance. In the short run, swimmers may need to be held to commitments, but in the long run—they need to want their own achievements.

Remember, particularly in the case of younger swimmers, attitude and behavior of the parents in regard to their outlook on the sport has an important effect on the child. In swimming, as in life, nobody can "win" or succeed all the time – there will be some inevitable disappointments. All children can gain from disappointments and successes alike. The important thing is to keep on striving to do better the next time.

The secret is to produce great swimmers - and to produce great young people who swim.

QUEST Fundraising

All fundraising accomplished by team families is specific to program enhancements for QUEST swimmers. This fundraising is done through QUEST Boosters, a non-profit 501c3 organization established and run by parents for the sole benefit of the swimmers; that is, funds raised do not go toward salaries or operational costs.

The primary fundraiser for Quest Boosters is the annual swim-a-thon and members are strongly encouraged to fully participate and support it. The amount of money raised during the swim-a-thon sets the budget for the Boosters for the following year and as such determines the amount of support that can be given back to families. Other smaller fundraisers, like Chik-fil-A Night and the use of scrip cards, are also run through the year.

There are many possibilities for the direction of funds that are raised and the Boosters Board makes those decisions. Some examples are:

- Practice equipment (unique, group-oriented)

- Uniform items

- Travel fund(s)

- Social activities

- Special awards events

Further, there are opportunities for philanthropic grants, individual giving, corporate sponsorships, special events, and other contributions that run the full measure of giving to a worthy cause.

Swimmers will graduate and move into further education and/or careers. A database of QUEST alumni should be maintained. Ongoing communications should occur with them. They should be recognized for their accomplishments into their professional lives. Hopefully, they will realize wonderful human benefits from being involved in the QUEST competitive program and some will be willing to contribute back to the program as they have the capability to do so.

Volunteering
QUEST does not have mandatory volunteer hours. However, QUEST could not provide the same quality experience for our swimmers without volunteers. There are many ways to get involved from serving as a meet buddy or group mentor to answering questions at an Open House to serving on the QUEST Boosters board. In addition, you will be asked to time lanes at meets by meet hosts.

COMMUNICATION

Communication is the cornerstone of all strong relationships. All best efforts will be made to keep you informed. It is hoped that you will provide the team with your comments and ideas. Due to the fact that we have different practice groups that swim at different times and in different pools, there is a need to have various forums for exchange of information. Therefore, several methods are established to ensure that information can be passed on and questions can be answered.

The Website

The website has a wealth of information on it to assist you. Specifically, look under Swim Team, What's New (bottom right corner), Events and Resources. You have to be logged in to view all of the available information under some of the tabs.

Parents' Meetings

During the swim season, parents' meetings will be held. The coaching staff will offer information on team philosophy, policy, and other areas which may be helpful to the parents. This forum is the place where the parents can learn more about the team as well as contribute new viewpoints. Specific times for the meetings will be emailed as well as being posted on the website and the pool bulletin board.

If you so desire, you may set up a specific time to meet with your child's coach.

Coaches' Notes

Periodically during the swim season, coaches' notes will be placed on the website. These notes will typically evaluate some seasonal period of time, recognize individuals for outstanding performance or contribution—and offer insights into the development of the team.

Emails

Email is the primary form of communication used at QUEST. You can add more than one email to your account to allow multiple members of the household to receive the same information. Emails are sent for practice changes, meet announcements, deadlines, and special events.

In addition, QUEST uses the Rained Out text alert system for short-notice, time-sensitive information. Sign up for both general alerts and alerts specific to your swimmers' group.

QUEST TRAINING PROGRAM

Team Placement and Progression

In keeping with the philosophy of providing a quality, competitive swimming program for young people of all ages, abilities, and levels of interest, QUEST offers different levels of professional instruction and training.

The broad categories are: Novice, Age Group, Senior

Within each category are three (3) levels:

Novice - QUEST 1, 2, 3

QUEST 1 – Mostly 7 and under – New to year-round competitive swimming.

Learning Skills – Introduce the idea of "the Art of Swimming," Rhythmic and Bi-lateral Breathing, Balance Points, Horizontal Body Lines, Body Length, Feel for the Water, Effective Kicking—in Freestyle, Backstroke, Breaststroke, and Butterfly, Individual Medley order, Starts, Turns, and Relays skills.

Learned skills performed over greater distance and less time.

Virginia Swimming meet formats and philosophy of competition; that is, racing is fun, we race <u>with</u> others not <u>against</u> others, using learned skills in races.

QUEST 2 – Mostly 8-10 years old - Continue perfecting learned skills from QUEST 1. An intended result is to begin to imprint appropriate movement patterns into the nervous system, for all of the four strokes, starts, turns, and relay participation. Greater emphasis on the Individual Medley as an event.

QUEST 3 – Mostly 9, 10 years old, some 11 years old – The expectation in QUEST 3 is that fundamentals have begun to be imprinted into the nervous system and that swimmers have a good understanding and sportsmanlike spirit for racing in practice - and in swim meets. Physically, swimmers show abilities to maintain fundamental techniques of some distance and time. Swimmers in this group are making a transition to be able to make a seamless adjustment to Age Group swimming.

Age Group

Age Group 1, 2, 3 – Age Group swimming is according to competition which happens in 2-year age categories. The categories are 9-10, 11-12, 13-14, 15-16, 17-18. Many meets categorize 15-18 together.

Age Group 1 – Mostly 11 – 12 years old, some 13 years old –
Freestyle: a commitment to bi-lateral breathing is given greater emphasis. Bi-lateral breathing creates symmetrical balance and rotation of the body from side to side, it establishes greater visibility to each side while practicing and racing, and it helps swimmers to perfect equal inhale and expulsion of air while swimming.

Note: There are differing opinions concerning the value of bi-lateral breathing and single-side breathing. At QUEST, we want swimmers to perfect the skill of bi-lateral breathing so that choices can be made later for individual swimmers regarding their best breathing methods and racing priorities.

Concepts further developed:

1. Breath: Rhythmic and full breathing.

2. A longer vessel is faster than a shorter vessel.

3. The use of balance points to use weight distribution for horizontal lines.

4. "My eyes give my brain the information it needs to tell my body what to do."

5. Effective kicking.

6. Energy systems and interval training are introduced as a norm in practice and racing.

7. Racing strategies for racing events are introduced and practiced.

All Strokes: Timing of the hips in concert with arms and legs is emphasized to create greater economy and power in movement.

Age Group 2 – Mostly 12 – 14 years old
Interval training and the practice of racing strategies transition to a level of sophistication at this level. Physiological considerations are planned to replicate the physiological challenges swimmers experience in championship meets when they compete in preliminary and finals sessions over 3 days or more.

We understand, proper technique is counterintuitive to most swimmers; therefore, planned attention to fundamentals of technique continues to be administered.

Age Group 3 – Mostly ages 13-16
This group transitions from age group swimming to senior swimming. They are normally experienced from novice 1 to age group 3; however, high school swimming has introduced swimmers with less competitive experience but who want to compete on their high school swim teams. These may begin the QUEST training program at Age Group 3.

Three (3) specific levels of training are introduced and used specifically at this stage. They are:

1. Aerobic Phase – Heart rates generally in the 140-160 range

2. VO2 Max Phase – Heart rates generally in the 160-180 range

3. Perk Performance Phase – Heart rates exceeding 180

Planned attention to technical perfection continues to be practiced.

Senior 1, 2, 3 – Mostly ages 13 – 18 years old
Senior
Senior swimming defined: Senior swimming is participation in USAS and international competition without regard to chronological age; that is, swimmers are qualified according to qualifying times and seeded according to their entered times.

At the highest levels of competition, World Championships and the Olympic Games, swimmers are chosen if they place in the top 2 in individual events and the top 6 in relay events. Other international meets are chosen similarly, such as the Pan Pacific Games, the Pan American Games, and the World University Games.

The Evolution of a Senior Swimmer
At some point, those swimmers who have reached the higher levels of age group swimming will confront the choice of continuing to compete at the age group level or to make "the leap" to senior swimming. This becomes a serious choice because of increased physical challenges, attention to the "mental game," and social limitations which are occasionally required specific to scheduling time – all elements of senior swimming.

Senior 1 – Swimmers at this level experience age group meets and senior meets as they transition - and learn - the differences. The daily time requirement for training is advanced and meets are scheduled for age group and senior competitive formats.

Senior 2 – The addition of two practice sessions on specified days are offered, and practice attendance at all practices is expected.

Senior 3 – Practically all meets are scheduled without regard for age categories; that is, swimmers compete on the basis of their achieved times, and they are seeded in meets accordingly. A 13-year-old might swim with a 20-year-old if their qualifying times for the meet are similar. Swimmers with goals of national and/or international competition normally practice in Senior 3.

Note: At high school ages, it is unusual - (but not impossible) - that swimmers qualify for international teams due to the fact that collegiate and professional swimmers have the following advantages:

1. Their physical statures have reached maturity.

2. They have more flexible time schedules to train and compete.

3. They have more experience in racing and training on which to depend.

However, USAS Club Swimming is a preparation for collegiate and professional programs and for the opportunities provided to graduating high school swimmers in their futures.

QUEST offers and provides these opportunities for swimmers so inclined. Our Senior 3 level of training will enable swimmers to endure successive multi-day, preliminary, and finals competitions - through to the final session of competition. It will also prepare QUEST swimmers to enter and succeed in any collegiate or professional program. These are the reasons for the expectations for practice attendance, discipline to group norms, and goal-setting practices at the Senior 3 level.

We often hear the statement: "It is lonely at the top." The statement is NOT actually true; however, there are fewer people who are willing to take the risks required to reach "the top." And – "the top" is a relative term because it has different meanings to different people. There are risks to advance to all new levels in life.

USA Olympic Trials is the most competitive swim meet in the world, yet there are at least 1,000 swimmers who compete in it. That is not a lonely circumstance.

Practice Attendance

Attendance Policies

There is a gradual progression in opportunities to practice as swimmers develop in ages and abilities. Swimmers are encouraged to attend the number of practices offered. That this is not possible for all swimmers all of the time is acknowledged. Year-round swimming from childhood to adult years means that flexibility is a necessity. Generally speaking, the best success can be expected by those who attend practice according to the plan.

QUEST I: Swimmers are encouraged to attend at least 2 practices per week.

QUEST II: Swimmers are encouraged to attend at least 3 practices per week.

QUEST 1: 2 Practices per week
QUEST 2: 3 Practices per week
QUEST 3: 3 – 5 Practices per week

AGE GROUP I, II, III: 4 – 6 Practices per week

SENIOR GROUPS:
Senior 1 – 6 Practices per week
Senior 2 – 6 to 8 Practices per week
Senior 3 – at least 9 Practices per week
Notes on Practice Expectations:

Always arrive at the pool at least 15 minutes prior to the start of practice so the most efficient use of the allotted time may be used.

Plan to stay the entire practice. The last of the practice is often a culmination of practice - and frequently when announcements are made.

When a swimmer cannot attend the recommended number of practices for their group, the coaches will discuss the situation with the swimmer and/or parents.

In case your swimmer will be out of the water for an extended period with an injury or illness, please notify the respective coach so that the coaching staff will be aware of the problem.

Occasionally, most of a practice group will be at a swim meet, in which case you will be notified of a practice change or cancellation of practice by email, text message, and/or the web site.

Try your best to do what the coaches are teaching.

Policies

Behavior

Swimmers are encouraged to support their teammates at practice as well as in competition. Working together as a unit for the benefit of all individuals in the group is an important part of the QUEST Spirit.

Always remember that both the parents and the swimmers represent QUEST. At away swim meets we are guests of the home team and should always respect their property and conduct ourselves properly.

QUEST swimmers are expected - at all times - to follow the oral and written directions of the coaching staff. At no time will disrespectful attitudes be tolerated from any swimmer.

Abusive language, lying, stealing, and/or vandalism are intolerable. These behaviors are directly contradictory to the objectives of QUEST and are detrimental enough to warrant strict disciplinary action; including suspension or dismissal if deemed necessary.

Swimmers may leave practice only with the coach's permission.

Swimmers and parents are expected to read, understand, and comply with all QUEST policies including but not limited to Anti-Bullying, Risky Behavior, and Electronic Communications

Electronic Communications

This includes cell phones, tablets, computers, smart devices, smart watches, virtual assistants, and any other device that communicates digitally. These are given special attention in this handbook because they have become a special behavior challenge at all places within society.

Swimmers, and people in general, are subject to poor and inappropriate behavior by this method like we have not experienced previously. Therefore –

THE FOLLOWING POLICIES ARE IN PLACE REGARDING THESE DEVICES AND APPLY TO BOTH SWIMMERS AND COACHES:

These devices may <u>not</u> be used at practices, meets, or on team travel, except to:

1. Listen to appropriate music. NO PROFANITY in the lyrics.

2. Make contact with a person according to need; that is, emergency, get picked up, deliver a specific message.

3. There can be no profanity or inappropriate viewing on YouTube, instant messaging, tweeting, Snapchat, websites, texting, Facebook, email, voice mail, etc. and all other types of communication that may come to us in the future.

Disconnecting from devices encourages personal interaction!

Team Uniform & Meet Procedures

All swimmers are required to wear the team suit and cap at swim meets. This promotes pride in our program. Wearing the team uniform (at a minimum, black QUEST t-shirt with black shorts/pants) enhances team spirit and affects the competition such that it is to the QUEST advantage. Swimmers may be scratched from events if they are not in team uniform.

QUEST is contracted with Arena Products. This means that we agree to wear Arena team suits for regular meets and Arena Tech suits for suitable competition, which for QUEST is Championship competitions or meets designated by the coaches. Arena, in return, gives certain benefits to swimmers that qualify for higher level championship competition and to coach's uniforms. This is mandatory for our swimmers per our contract. It is not negotiable.

We use Arena because the look differentiates our uniform from others within our marketplace.

Our outfitter for Arena products and for equipment is Swim and Tri Swim Shop. Please use Swim and Tri whenever possible.

Also available through QUEST Boosters are t-shirts, sweats, shorts, jackets, baseball caps, and more - all imprinted with the QUEST logo. It is highly recommended that the swimmers name be placed on all parts of the team uniform.

All swimmers entered in a meet are required to participate in the warm-up session. Swimmers should arrive at the pool 20 minutes prior to the warm-up time. Coaches announcements, team spirit drills, stretching, becoming familiar with the pool, and physical preparation for racing occur between arrival time and the completion of the warm-up period. Swimmers who are repeatedly late or who miss the warm-up time may lose the privilege of competing, at the discretion of the coaches.

Practice Equipment

All practice groups are expected to be at their designated starting place, with their practice equipment, ready to start practice on time. Standard equipment for all groups is a swim suit (any make or color), QUEST cap, goggles, and swim fins. Additional equipment may be required for advanced practice groups and will be sent out and is listed in the Frequently Asked Questions on the website under Swim Team (you have to be logged in to view it).

Pool Rules

The following rules and regulations are for the benefit and protection of all pool users.

- Persons with contagious or infectious skin conditions will not be admitted.

- Proper swim wear is required; no jeans, shirts, cutoffs, or gym shorts are permitted.

- THERE IS NO SMOKING OR VAPING OR E-CIGARETTES ALLOWED ON ANY QUEST PROPERTY.

- No breakable containers or metal objects are allowed in the pool area.

- No swimmer allowed in the water unless a coach is on deck.

Philosophy of Competition

Competitive meets are opportunities to elevate personal and team potential. The purpose of competition is to enhance each swimmer's extension toward his or her performance potential and collectively that of the team.

"The Race" is the fun because it takes us higher within ourselves, not because it takes us higher than others. The competition causes our mental focus to become most keen, causes our spirit to soar to elevated levels, and causes our bodies to surpass normal expectations. This allows us to venture toward ultimate potential and peak performance. No person could realize one's dreams without one's competitors. Competitors are to be valued and respected for this reason. Competitors must be treated in a sportsmanlike fashion.

QUEST swimmers are trained and encouraged to compete in all swimming events, distances, and strokes. This policy promotes versatility and encourages swimmers to explore their potential in the wide range of events offered in competitive swimming.

Pyramid of Participation

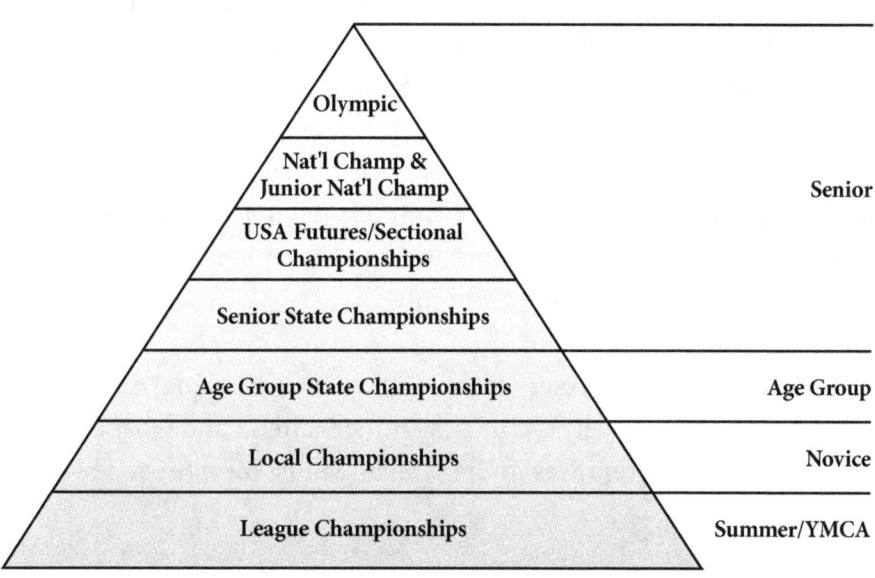

It is said that the ancient pyramids were powerful and strong because the placement of each piece in the structure was critical to the standing of the entire structure. And so it is with the pyramid of participation in the sport of club swimming. The entry levels of development are at the base of the swimming pyramid. Swimmers at this stage are larger in number and they provide support (energy and financial) for athletes who have achieved higher performance levels, but are fewer in number. However, the few at the top of the pyramid are also important because their performances become the achievement standards (goals) for developmental swimmers. For the full power of the pyramid to be realized, all levels of development are essential.

Meet Schedule

A meet schedule is established to give each swimmer the chance to race and to measure their performance levels. It is also an opportunity to be evaluated for their effectiveness. Participation is necessary for the individual and for teammates.

The meet schedule for each season will be distributed at the beginning of the season. The meet schedule has been established with expectations that the swimmers will attend meets approximately once per month. On average, coaches will expect swimmers to compete every three to four weeks. In some cases, meets of a similar classification (i.e., "B-C" meet) are scheduled as close as two weeks or as far as one month apart. This happens when the meets available to us offer no alternative. When swimmers begin to qualify up, they may race more than once a month during championship season (December, February/March, and July).

The coaching staff reserves the right to make the final decision concerning which meets QUEST swimmers attend and what events they swim. Any exceptions to the schedule must be approved by the coaching staff.

Team championship meets are indicated on the meet schedule. Since Championship meets are considered to be culminating activities, swimmers who are qualified to swim are expected to attend these meets and contribute to the total team effort. The Virginia DISTRICT, REGIONAL, AND STATE Championships are always considered team efforts. There are no qualifying times for the district and regional championships.

Swim Meet Entry Procedure

An email will be sent when registration for a meet opens. Parents must opt in or out of the meet (declare to attend or decline to attend) before the deadline.

Parents will select the events desired but coaches have the final say in what events are entered.

Put notes in the note section of the entry file if desired. A note could be that the swimmer is unavailable on a specific day to swim or has to depart early for instance.

Read the meet invitation for information about the number of events allowed per session/day and the order of events.

QUEST philosophy is to swim the maximum number of events allowed in the meet invite if the swimmer is capable of doing so. Novice swimmers may not be able to do the max number initially.

Coaches will enter the relays. It is considered a privilege to compete in a relay for QUEST.

Financial Obligations

New Swimmer trial period
New swimmers may try the Quest program for 2 weeks without financial obligation. After the two week trial period, they must join QUEST and USA Swimming. Insurance prohibits swimmers from participating in a QUEST Swimming, Inc., activity without being a member of USA Swimming.

Financial terms of membership
Your swim fees are based on an annual contract between QUEST and the swimming family. QUEST offers several different options for

payment. You can pay in full, or in installments with a 15% deposit downpayment (Refer to your QUEST contract for a full description of payment options plus Terms and Conditions.)

If your account is not current by the 5th of each month, you will be subject to a late payment charge of $50. If fees are 3 months past due, swimmers will not be permitted to practice or swim in meets. At that time, families will have 30 days to resolve the outstanding debt before dismissal from the team.

Swimmers joining prior to October 1 will pay full membership fees. Swimmers joining on or after October 1 will pay on a pro-rated basis. The swimming year begins on or about September 1 and runs through approximately August 15.

Refunds

Typically refunds are not granted. When a swimmer's participation is officially terminated, billing will be stopped effective the first day of the following month.

Termination Notification

Our goal is that your swimmer will have a long, enjoyable experience with QUEST that lasts through high school (and maybe beyond).

If you are considering terminating your membership at QUEST, please meet with a coach prior to leaving the program.

Should you decide to leave QUEST please fill out this form.

Your feedback is appreciated and can help make QUEST better.

Should you find it necessary to discontinue swimming with QUEST please take a minute to return this exit form so we can be sure to refund fees, if applicable, and notify coaches of the termination, if you have not already done so.

Swimmer Name(s): _____

Practice Group(s): _____

Reason for leaving: _____

_____

_____

_____

_____

_____

_____

_____

Parent Signature: _____

Date: _____

Return to:
coachjohn@questswimming.com
OR
QUEST
6800 Deer Run Drive
Midlothian, VA 23112

Appendix B — A Typical Day in 2003

A typical day in 2003:
MONDAY/WEDNESDAY/FRIDAY

Wake up	2:30 a.m.
Stretch	15 minutes – 2:45 a.m.
Shower/shave	2:50 – 3:10 a.m.
Dress, pour coffee & leave	3:30 a.m.
Arrive at pool	4:00 a.m.
Check pool, Practice set up	
Begin Practice	4:30 a.m. (M W F)
Senior Practice	4:30 – 6:30 a.m.
Novice Practice	6:30 – 7:45 a.m.
Clean Building	8:00 – 9:00 a.m. (bathrooms, front room, hallway, pump room, office - breakfast)
Masters Practice	9:00 – 10:30 a.m.
Office	10:30 am - 12:30 p.m. (check money, check email/voice mail, phone calls & practice planning, etc.)
Lunch	12:30 – 1:00 p.m. (power nap - time permitting)
Grounds	1:30 – 3:30 p.m. (pool chemicals, pool vacuum, blow deck area, Cut grass on the property, etc.)
Practice	3:30 – 8:45 p.m. (normally I did dry land with swimmers for exercise)
Clean Building	9:00 – 10:00 p.m.
Arrive home	10:45 p.m.
Sleep	11:30 pm – 2:30 a.m.

TUESDAY/THURSDAY/SATURDAY

Wake up	5:30 a.m.
Stretch	15 minutes – 5:45 a.m.
Shower/Shave	5:45 – 6:05 a.m.
Dress, pour coffee, & leave	6:30 a.m.
Arrive at pool	7:00 a.m.
Breakfast & Office Work	7:00 – 8:00 a.m. (This occasionally took more time)
Check Pool & Maintenance	8:00 – 10:00 a.m. (More or Less)
Office	10:00 – Noon
Lunch	Noon – 12:30 p.m.
General Needs	12:45 – 3:00 p.m.
Practices	3:30 – 8:45 p.m.
Clean Building	9:00 – 10:00 p.m.
Arrive Home	10:45 p.m.

SATURDAY AFTERNOONS & SUNDAYS

Miscellaneous home or pool.
Swim Meets on certain scheduled weekends.

I lived 30 minutes from the pool in 2003. I moved within 12 minutes of the pool in 2004 which added about 20 minutes in the morning and 20 minutes at night to my sleep time.

This schedule was in the first year of ownership when I worked alone. I hired John Smithson in 2004. He added significant flexibility to my time.

As years passed, staff was hired. We now have almost 25 coaches and instructors on staff.

These were typical work days; however, there were meetings and miscellaneous work that I would fit in as needed. I maintained some limited presence at SwimMetro Management, Inc., as majority owner and swim lessons instructor training. This work reduced significantly to nil within the first 3 years.

Home life was practically nil as well during the first year of operations. There was more time for home and family as the years passed.

The pool property was not terribly old but it had not been maintained well for some years. It seemed there were items to improve or repair most of the time in the early years. SwimMetro was a huge help in this regard.

My mindset was to do whatever it took to succeed with the team and with the business. I never minded cleaning the facilities or working on the property. It is interesting that when I told myself to do the work, I was altogether okay with it, and I did it for no compensation; however, when other people told me to do similar type work, I would weigh the worth based on time and compensation.

Thinking back, I wonder how I managed it all, and I'm sure I did not manage everything so well. But I am surely glad that I had the opportunity, and took it, to own the property and the business.

About The Author

Dudley Duncan is a retired club swimming coach from Virginia. He has coached club swimming for multiple clubs starting with the Bounty Otters Swim Club (now Old Dominion AC), Indian River Community College Club program, Tritons of Petersburg, Poseidon Swimming, and Quest Swimming.

In 2003, he purchased his own pool property and began his own club swimming team, Quest Swimming.

Duncan was inducted into the International Swim Coaches Association (ISCA) Hall of Fame (2017), the Virginia Swimming Hall of Fame (2019), the SwimRVA Hall of Inspiration (2022), and the American Swim Coaches Hall of Fame (2023).

He currently resides in Vero Beach, Florida, with his wife, Jeannie, and their sheepadoodle, Vero.

Acknowledgments

I would like to acknowledge the sacrifices of the traditional family time which many families experience, made by my family (Jeannie, Julie and Ryan); that is, before and after school day/work day hours when fathers are typically home, weekends and holidays. This is true for my immediate family and for my extended family as it relates to vacations and holidays for which I was absent (mostly). Club coaching is "almost" all consuming intellectually, emotionally, physically and spiritually. In striving for excellence in club coaching, I know the sacrifices you made for my career and the way I did it.

ALL of the staff members who shared my experience as a club coach were my teammates in leading efforts for excellence. Any and All recognition I have experienced has been dependent on THEIR work plus ALL SWIMMERS on the respective teams who swam for excellence and became better athletes altogether. They were and are the essence of the Art of Swimming and the Game of Racing.

Anastasia Carneal, the Lead Instructor of the Quest Swim School, drew the illustrations used in this book. She made the words around them come to life and gave better understanding to an unknown sum of people who see them.

The CG sports Management, Inc. team, specific to the publishing segment of the business, turned the roughly described thoughts of a 51 year coaching career into this presentation of it.

Taylor Brien - Editor - Kept a reasonable source of continuity to so many elements of consideration as they relate to club coaching. She understood on so many levels, she improved my descriptions of those elements and she was entirely patient in many long discussions to elucidate the concepts within the book.

Nicole Wurtele - Book Designer - Took the edited manuscript and put it into book form. She also provided the interesting "reflection" photograph which became the cover of the book. In fact, the photograph motivated me to change the subtitle of the book. Originally it was Perspectives of a ..... and we changed it to Reflections of a .... to draw continuity between the cover and the subtitle.

Michael (Mike) Nicloy - Sound and Publishing—Produced the audio book and elements of the book design. I flew to Wisconsin to use Mike's sound studio and to benefit from his guidance. This was another unique experience and for which I was "without a clue." Mike made the experience seem natural and relaxed.

Cejih Yung - As the owner of CG Sports Management, Inc., Cejih was the leader in the process from start to finish - and was integral to presenting the book to the public.

I would like to thank Chuck Warner for providing "author insights" and directing me in my search for a publisher.

It has been said to me on numerous occasions: "You should write a book." Those people motivated me and I am thankful for their confidence in me to do this.

THANK YOU EVERYBODY!

www.ingramcontent.com/pod-product-compliance
Lightning Source LLC
Chambersburg PA
CBHW060916120626
46553CB00001B/346